Exploring Music History

A Guided Approach

Generously donated by
Wanda Petzschler

VOLUME 2

MIDDLE AGES TO CLASSICAL

by
Janet Lopinski, Joe Ringhofer,
and Peteris Zarins

National Library of Canada Cataloguing in Publication Data

Lopinski, Janet Marie
   Exploring music history : a guided approach / Janet Lopinski, Joe Ringhofer,
   Peteris Zarins.

Contents: v. 1. Baroque to the modern era – v. 2. Middle ages to classical –
v. 3. 19th and 20th centuries.
ISBN 0-88797-824-X (v. 1). – ISBN 0-88797-826-6 (v. 2). – ISBN 0-88797-783-9 (v. 3).

1. Music – History and criticism – Instruction and study – Activity programs.
2. Music – History and criticism – Problems, exercises, etc.
I. Ringhofer, Joe J. II. Zarins, Peteris III. Title.

ML193.L748 2002   780'.9   C2002-900878-6

© Copyright 2002 The Frederick Harris Music Co., Limited
All Rights Reserved

ISBN 0-88797-826-6

Contents

Preface 6

Unit One — Four Eras of Music History 8
Timeline: Overview of the Four Eras 8
Historical and Cultural Background 8
    Middle Ages 8
    Renaissance 11
    Supplemental Activity: Looking at Renaissance Art 13
    Baroque 14
    Classical 15
    Supplemental Activity: Identifying Historical Events 16

Review and Reflection 19
Quiz 20

Unit Two — Sacred Vocal Music of the Middle Ages and Renaissance 21
Timeline 21
GREGORIAN CHANT 21
    Building a Musical Vocabulary: Gregorian Chant 22
    Supplemental Activity: Identifying Modes 23
    Required Listening: Anonymous, *Haec dies* (Chant) 24
    Hildegard of Bingen 26

ORGANUM 27
    Origins: Early Polyphony 27
    Building a Musical Vocabulary: Organum 28
    Notre Dame School: Léonin and Pérotin 28
    Required Listening: Anonymous, *Haec dies* (Organum) 29

MOTET 30
    Origins: 13th-century Motet 30
    Building a Musical Vocabulary: 13th-century Motet 31
    Required Listening: Anonymous, *O mitissima/Virgo/Haec dies* 31
    14th-century Motet 32
    15th-century Motet 33
    Building a Musical Vocabulary: 15th-century Motet 33
    Josquin des Prez 33
    Required Listening: Josquin, *Ave Maria...virgo serena* 34
    Supplemental Activity: Comparing a 13th- and 15th-century Motet 35

MASS 36
    Building a Musical Vocabulary: Mass 36
    The Reformation and Counter-Reformation 37
    Giovanni Pierluigi da Palestrina 38
    Required Listening: Palestrina, "Gloria" from *Pope Marcellus Mass* 38

Review and Reflection 40
Quiz 41

UNIT THREE — Secular Vocal Music of the Middle Ages and Renaissance 42

Timeline 42

CHANSON 43

Building a Musical Vocabulary: Chanson 43
Required Listening: Moniot d'Arras, *Ce fut en mai* 44
The 14th-century *Ars Nova* 46
Guillaume de Machaut 46
Required Listening: Machaut, *Puis qu'en oubli* 47

MADRIGAL 49

Building a Musical Vocabulary: Madrigal 49
Italian Madrigal 50
Required Listening: Carlo Gesualdo, *Moro lasso, al mio duolo* 50
English Madrigal 53
Required Listening: Farmer, *Fair Phyllis I Saw Sitting All Alone* 54
Supplemental Activity: Learning about Elizabeth I 57

Review and Reflection 57
Quiz 58

UNIT FOUR — Vocal Music of the Baroque and Classical Eras 59

Timeline 59

OPERA 59

Origins: Florentine Camerata 59
Building a Musical Vocabulary: Opera 61
Claudio Monteverdi 62
Required Listening: Monteverdi, *The Coronation of Poppea* (Coronation Scene) . 63
Henry Purcell 67
Required Listening: Purcell, *Dido and Aeneas* (Final Scene) 67
Handel and Italian Opera in England 70
Gluck and Operatic Reform 70
Building a Musical Vocabulary: Classical Opera 71
Wolfgang Amadeus Mozart 72
Required Listening: Mozart, *The Marriage of Figaro* (Selections from Act One) 72
Supplemental Activity: Viewing a Complete Performance
   of *The Marriage of Figaro* 77

CANTATA 77

Building a Musical Vocabulary: Cantata 78
Johann Sebastian Bach 79
Required Listening: Bach, *Cantata No. 80*, "Ein feste Burg ist unser Gott"
   (Selections) 79

ORATORIO 84
    Building a Musical Vocabulary: Oratorio 84
    Franz Joseph Haydn 84
    Required Listening: Haydn, *The Creation* (Selections) 84
    Recommended Listening for Oratorio 88
    Supplemental Activity: "The Movies Go to the Opera" 88

Review and Reflection 89
Quiz 90

UNIT FIVE — Instrumental Music of the Middle Ages, Renaissance, and Baroque 91

Timeline 91

The Role of Instrumental Music in the Middle Ages and Renaissance 91
Indoor and Outdoor Instruments 92

DANCE MUSIC 94
    Building a Musical Vocabulary: Dance Music 94
    Required Listening: Anonymous, *Royal Estampie No. 4* from
        Chansonnier du Roy 95
    Music Publishing in the Renaissance 96
    Tielman Susato and *Danserye* 97
    Required Listening: Pavane "Mille regretz" AND Ronde I and Ronde II
        (from *Danserye*) 97
    Supplemental Activity: Listening to the Chanson "Mille regretz" 100

KEYBOARD MUSIC 101
    Building a Musical Vocabulary: Early Keyboard Instruments 101
    The *Fitzwilliam Virginal Book* 102
    Building a Musical Vocabulary: Early Keyboard Genres 103
    Domenico Scarlatti 103
    Required Listening: Scarlatti, *Sonata in D Minor*, L 413, K 9 OR
        Sonata in D Major, L 463, K 430 104
    Supplemental Activity: Exploring the Artistry of Glenn Gould 105

SUITE 106
    Building a Musical Vocabulary: Baroque Dance Suite 106
    George Frideric Handel 108
    Required Listening: Handel, *Water Music* (Selections) 108

CONCERTO 112
    Building a Musical Vocabulary: Baroque Concerto 112
    Johann Sebastian Bach 113
    Required Listening: Bach, *Brandenburg Concerto No. 2 in F Major*, BWV 1047 113
    Recommended Listening for Baroque Concerto 115
    Supplemental Activity: Comparing Baroque and Modern Performance Practice 116

Review and Reflection 117
Quiz 118

UNIT SIX — **Instrumental Music of the Classical Era** 119

Timeline 119

SYMPHONY 119

- C.P.E. Bach and the Pre-Classical Style 119
- Building a Musical Vocabulary: Symphony 121
- Wolfgang Amadeus Mozart 123
- Required Listening: Mozart, *Symphony No. 40 in G Minor*, K 550 123
- Franz Joseph Haydn 127
- Required Listening: Haydn, *Symphony No. 104 in D Major* ("London") 127

SONATA 131

- Ludwig van Beethoven 131
- Required Listening: Beethoven, *Sonata in C Minor*, op. 13 ("Pathétique") 132
- Supplemental Activity: Comparing Sonata Recordings 139

CONCERTO 141

- Building a Musical Vocabulary: Classical Concerto 141
- Wolfgang Amadeus Mozart 141
- Required Listening: Mozart, *Piano Concerto in G Major*, K 453 142
- Supplemental Activity: Sampling Additional Concertos 147

CHAMBER MUSIC 148

- Building a Musical Vocabulary: Chamber Music 148
- Franz Schubert 149
- Required Listening: Schubert, *Piano Quintet in A Major* ("Trout") 149

Review and Reflection 153
Quiz 154

Final Summary and Review 155

APPENDICES

Appendix A – Recommended Resources 158
  Dictionaries and Encyclopedias; General Texts; Middle Ages Texts;
  Renaissance Period Texts; Baroque Period Texts; Classical Period Texts;
  Internet Resources; Video Resources (VHS and DVD)
Appendix B – Recommended Listening Materials 161
Appendix C – Listening Report 164

Preface

This book is the second of a three-volume series entitled *Exploring Music History: A Guided Approach*. These three workbooks are intended to support students and teachers preparing for The Royal Conservatory of Music (RCM) history examinations as outlined in the *Theory Syllabus, 2002 edition*. They will also be useful to students whose goal is simply to explore music history for the sake of becoming better informed as musicians and listeners.

Volume 2 explores the development of major genres in Western art music, beginning with Gregorian chant and concluding with the Classical symphony. For students following the RCM History curriculum, this volume is intended to prepare candidates for the Grade 4 History Examination. You may wonder why we begin this journey with music so far removed from our everyday experience, when the repertoire we perform usually starts with the works of J.S. Bach and his contemporaries. While we sometimes think of Baroque music as a starting point, it is actually a high point in hundreds of years of development. Our appreciation of fugues by Bach, concertos by Vivaldi, and arias by Handel will be more complete when we understand these genres in the context of what came before them. For this reason, this book traces the evolution of selected genres from the Gothic era to the birth of the Industrial Age.

This is not a textbook. We assume that students will be working with an introductory music history or music appreciation textbook, using music dictionaries or encyclopedias, doing internet research, and/or attending lectures or classes given by a qualified teacher. We also expect that students will listen to recordings of the works studied—not doing so would be like studying art history without viewing a single painting! Whenever possible, it would be beneficial for students to examine musical scores while completing listening activities. For a list of recommended resources that includes books, encyclopedias, websites, videos, and DVDs, please consult Appendix A. Appendix B lists recommended listening materials for all required pieces in this volume.

This volume contains a variety of activities that require both writing and listening. Terms necessary to understand and describe music are introduced in segments entitled "Building a Musical Vocabulary." (If this is your first experience studying music history, please consult Volume 1 of this series for an introduction to the materials of music.) For each new genre, introductory information is presented. Specific compositions to be studied in detail are identified by the heading "Required Listening." We have also provided recommendations for additional listening, as well as a template for listening reports that can be assigned as homework (see Appendix C). At the end of each unit, a section entitled "Review and Reflection" helps students synthesize the information presented and invites personal opinions. Each unit concludes with a short quiz.

Since we believe that the study of music history can and should be both interesting and enjoyable, we have included additional items and activities designed to enrich the learning experience and give students a broader perspective. The heading "Did You Know?" is used to present interesting or unusual facts and stories. Computer-savvy students are invited to use the internet in "Web Quests." The heading "Supplemental Activity" is used for additional tasks such as completing diagrams, doing comparative listening, watching films, and viewing artwork.

We hope that upon completing this book, students will have developed a familiarity with the musical styles and most significant genres of the Middle Ages, Renaissance, Baroque, and Classical eras, and as a result, perform music—and listen to it—with deeper understanding.

Janet Lopinski, Joe Ringhofer, Peteris Zarins

Acknowledgements

The authors would like to thank the following people for their valuable assistance in preparing this publication:

Dr. Laura Beauchamp, Editor
Dr. Trish Sauerbrei, Editor-in-Chief, The Frederick Harris Music Co., Limited
Jennifer de Boer, Project Administrator

UNIT ONE

FOUR ERAS OF MUSIC HISTORY

Every successful journey requires careful preparation. As we embark on our exploration of musical genres from the Middle Ages, Renaissance, Baroque, and Classical eras, we should first have an overview of the cultural and historical events from each period.

Examine the timeline below. Which terms are already familiar to you?

Timeline

A.D. 476	1450	1600	1750	1825
MIDDLE AGES	**RENAISSANCE**	**BAROQUE**	**CLASSICAL**	
Early Christian Romanesque Gothic Ars Nova			Pre-Classical Rococo	

Historical and Cultural Background

Middle Ages (ca 476-1450)

Historians frequently regard the Middle Ages as a period framed by the fall of the Roman Empire (A.D. 476) and the fall of Constantinople (1453). This broad era spans approximately one thousand years, but is often broken down into specific periods as shown on the timeline (Early Christian, Gothic, etc.).

Many people associate the Middle Ages with stories about King Arthur, and with images of chivalry and knighthood. The Roman Catholic Church also had a strong influence on virtually all aspects of European life, including music.

Look up the term *medieval* in a dictionary. Why is it appropriate to use this term in reference to the Middle Ages?

_____

_____

_____

Why is the term *Dark Ages* used in reference to the early years of this era?

_____

_____

_____

Volume 2: Middle Ages to Classical   Exploring Music History: A Guided Approach

What does the term *Romanesque* signify?

_____

_____

_____

What does the term *Gothic* signify?

_____

_____

_____

Provide dates for the leading historical and cultural figures listed below and comment briefly on their significance.

Boethius (_480_ – _524_) _Philosopher and mathematician whose treatise De institutione musica is the most important source of information on music of this era._

Charlemagne (_____–_____) _____

_____

_____

William the Conqueror (_____–_____) _____

_____

_____

Eleanor of Aquitaine (_____–_____) _____

_____

_____

Richard the Lion-Hearted (_____–_____) _____

_____

_____

Kublai Khan (_____–_____) _____

_____

_____

Marco Polo (_____–_____) _____

_____

_____

Dante Alighieri (_____–_____) _____
_____
_____

Geoffrey Chaucer (_____–_____) _____
_____
_____

Joan of Arc (_____–_____) _____
_____
_____

Explain the role of monasticism and monastic life in the Middle Ages.
_____
_____
_____

Why are the Middle Ages sometimes referred to as the "Age of Chivalry"?
_____
_____
_____

What was the feudal system and how was it different from the way in which our modern society functions?
_____
_____
_____

What was the "Black Death" and what impact did it have on medieval society?
_____
_____
_____

WEB QUEST — What do you think the daily lives of ordinary people your age were like in the Middle Ages? How did they dress? What did they eat? What were their homes like? You can find interesting information about Medieval life on the internet. Start your exploration by entering "Daily life in the Middle Ages" into a search engine.

Renaissance (ca 1450-1600)

The French word *renaissance* is used to designate a period in European history roughly spanning the years 1450–1600. Literally, the term means "rebirth," which might make us wonder: a rebirth of what?

A decisive break with the past took place in the Renaissance, a past in which thought and action were governed largely by church practices. Renaissance individuals sought to free themselves from the restrictive views of the Roman Catholic Church by turning to science for fresh answers to life's mysteries. People began to embrace new ways of thinking by looking at life in more secular ways. The Church would remain an important force throughout the Renaissance, but one whose influence was increasingly limited to the spiritual realm.

Historians often refer to the Renaissance Era as the Age of Humanism. What intellectual currents from this period would support this designation?

_____

_____

_____

_____

_____

_____

Provide dates for the leading historical and cultural figures listed below and comment briefly on their significance:

Johann Gutenberg (_____–_____) _____

_____

Ottavio de' Petrucci (_____–_____) _____

_____

Philip the Good (_____–_____) _____
and
Charles the Bold (_____–_____) _____
(Dukes of Burgundy)

_____

Christopher Columbus (_____–_____) _____

_____

Martin Luther (_____–_____) _____

Henry VIII of England (_____–_____) _____

Elizabeth I of England (_____–_____) _____

William Shakespeare (_____–_____) _____

Niccolo Machiavelli (_____–_____) _____

Nicolaus Copernicus (_____–_____) _____

Erasmus of Rotterdam (_____–_____) _____

Nostradamus (_____–_____) _____

Galileo Galilei (_____–_____) _____

Supplemental Activity: *Looking at Renaissance Art*

By exploring some of the key artistic figures of the Renaissance, you will gain a better understanding of the stylistic and philosophical streams that characterized the era. Using art books or the internet, locate at least one famous work by each of the leading figures listed below, and then briefly record your impressions. You may want to consider these questions: What is being depicted? Is the subject matter sacred or secular? How has the artist conveyed the human or personal element? What words would you use to describe the work: serene, dramatic, pastoral, domestic?

Giovanni Bellini (_____–_____)

Title of work _____

Your impression _____

_____

Sandro Botticelli (_____–_____)

Title of work _____

Your impression _____

_____

Hieronymous Bosch (_____–_____)

Title of work _____

Your impression _____

_____

Leonardo da Vinci (_____–_____)

Title of work _____

Your impression _____

_____

Michelangelo Buonarotti (_____–_____)

Title of work _____

Your impression _____

_____

Albrecht Dürer (_____–_____)

Title of work _____

Your impression _____

_____

Raphael Sanzio (_____–_____)

Title of work _____

Your impression _____

_____

 How do you think the lives of people in the Renaissance were different from the lives of people in the Middle Ages? In what ways did the many inventions and discoveries of the era impact everyday life? Using the phrase "Life in the Renaissance," search the internet for information on this subject.

Baroque (ca 1600-1750)

The period designated as the Baroque was marked by turbulence and contrast. It was the age of discovery and reason, yet also the era of absolute monarchy and religious conflict. There was both opulent wealth and abject poverty. These divergent characteristics were reflected in the arts and culture of the period.

The term "Baroque" itself is revealing. It is derived from the Portuguese *barroco*, which means "oddly shaped pearl." The misshapen pearl can serve as a metaphor for the conflicting forces that were at work. Dramatic subject matter, vivid colors, violent images, and intricate ornamentation in particular marked the visual arts in the Baroque era.

The Baroque period also witnessed significant developments in the fields of mathematics, science, and medicine. These advancements and broadening insights gave rise to new currents in philosophy.

Provide dates for the leading historical and cultural figures listed below and comment briefly on their significance:

Peter Paul Rubens (_____–_____) _____

_____

_____

René Descartes (_____–_____) _____

_____

_____

Rembrandt van Rijn (_____–_____) _____

_____

_____

Louis XIV (_____–_____) _____

_____

_____

Isaac Newton (_____–_____) _____

_____

_____

William Harvey (_____–_____) _____

_____

_____

Jean-Baptiste Molière (_____–_____) _____

_____

_____

Johann Kepler (_____–_____) _____

_____

_____

WEB QUEST — Nowhere is the grandeur and splendor of the Baroque style more evident than in the palaces constructed in this era. Using a search engine, explore websites dedicated to Baroque palaces, including Versailles, Sanssouci, Ludwigsburg, and Pamphili. Notice the scale of construction, the elaborate ornamentation, and the unparalleled luxury.

Classical (ca 1750-1825)

Historians often refer to the late 18th century as the Age of Enlightenment. This was an era characterized by the pursuit of knowledge, rational thinking, and a growing desire for equality among all people. Over time, the ornate and opulent style of the Baroque era was replaced by the Classical ideals of proportion, symmetry, and balance. Musicians, artists, and architects in this era took their inspiration from the simplicity and clean lines of Greco-Roman architectural models.

Provide dates for the leading historical and cultural figures listed below and comment briefly on their significance:

Jean-Jacques Rousseau (_____–_____) _____

_____

_____

Exploring Music History: A Guided Approach — Volume 2: Middle Ages to Classical

Voltaire (_____-_____) _____

_____

_____

Benjamin Franklin (_____-_____) _____

_____

_____

William Blake (_____-_____) _____

_____

_____

Thomas Jefferson (_____-_____) _____

_____

_____

Edward Jenner (_____-_____) _____

_____

_____

James Watt (_____-_____) _____

_____

_____

Vienna, the capital of Austria, was a leading cosmopolitan center in the late 18th century. This vibrant city stood at the crossroads between Europe and the East, and attracted the leading artists, architects, writers, and musicians of the day. Use your search engine and the phrase "Eighteenth-Century Vienna" to learn more about the role this progressive and dynamic city played during the Classical era.

Supplemental Activity: *Identifying Historical Events*

Using the resources of your choice (encyclopedia, history book, or internet) look up the following events and comment on their impact. Provide the date that each took place, and then unscramble the events by placing them in chronological order on the timeline provided. Once the timeline is complete, add to each era two additional events or historical figures of interest to you.

French Revolution _1789_

Initiated the downfall of the last King and Queen of France, Louis XVI and Marie Antoinette; "Liberty, Equality, and Fraternity" became the rallying cry of the revolutionaries.

Signing of the Magna Carta _____

_____

_____

The Great Fire of London _____

_____

_____

Spanish Inquisition _____

_____

_____

The Mayflower reaches Plymouth Rock _____

_____

_____

The Crusades _____

_____

_____

Execution of Charles I _____

_____

_____

Wars of the Roses _____

_____

_____

American Revolution _____

_____

_____

The Hundred Years War _____

_____

_____

Timeline

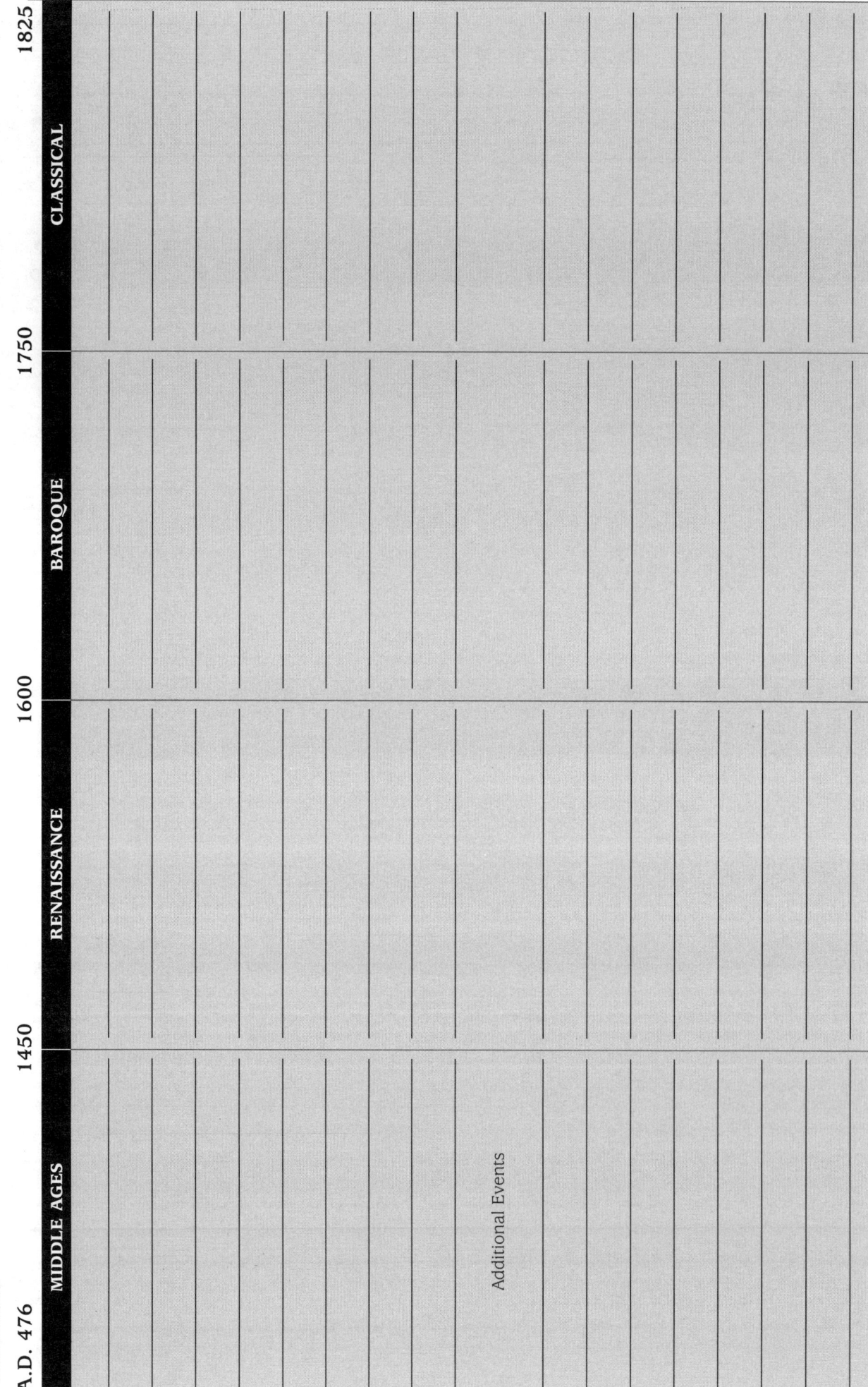

Note: Remember to add to each era two additional events or historical figures of interest to you.

Review and Reflection

Based on your introduction to the Middle Ages, Renaissance, Baroque, and Classical eras, what do you think the life of a musician was like in each of the four periods? What type of work was available for musicians? What challenges did they face? Who did they work for? What role did patrons play in their careers?

Middle Ages

_____
_____
_____
_____
_____

Renaissance

_____
_____
_____
_____
_____

Baroque

_____
_____
_____
_____
_____

Classical

_____
_____
_____
_____
_____

Quiz

For each of the four historical eras below, give approximate dates and name one historical event, one political figure or ruler, one artist, and one writer:

Middle Ages

Approximate dates _____

Historical figure _____

Political figure or ruler _____

Artist _____

Writer _____

Renaissance

Approximate dates _____

Historical figure _____

Political figure or ruler _____

Artist _____

Writer _____

Baroque

Approximate dates _____

Historical figure _____

Political figure or ruler _____

Artist _____

Writer _____

Classical

Approximate dates _____

Historical figure _____

Political figure or ruler _____

Artist _____

Writer _____

UNIT TWO

SACRED VOCAL MUSIC OF THE MIDDLE AGES AND RENAISSANCE

Timeline

	850	1150	1300	1450	1600
A.D. 476		**MIDDLE AGES**		**RENAISSANCE**	
Dark Ages	Romanesque	Gothic	Ars Nova		
GENRES					
Gregorian chant ···					
Mass ···					
	Early Polyphony: Organum ·····································				
		Motet ··			
COMPOSERS					
"Anonymous" ···································					
	Hildegard of Bingen				
	Notre Dame School				
			Guillaume de Machaut		
				Josquin des Prez	
				Giovanni Pierluigi da Palestrina	

Gregorian Chant

In contrast with the rich oral traditions of other world cultures, the evolution of Western art music is closely tied to the development of a rather elaborate system of notation. It seems appropriate to begin our journey with the earliest attempt to document music in the Western world: *Gregorian chant*.

Gregorian chant represents the earliest form of notated music in the Western tradition. Gregorian chants are monophonic, modal melodies with unmeasured rhythm and Latin text. Besides serving as functional music in the worship services of the Roman Catholic Church, these chants were used as the basis for many new compositions during the Middle Ages and Renaissance.

Who was Pope Gregory the Great and why is his name linked to this genre?

_____

_____

_____

_____

The terms *plainchant* and *plainsong* refer to a large body of chants from many different regions and traditions. Some other types of chant besides Gregorian include: Ambrosian, named after St. Ambrose, Bishop of Milan; Gallican, from Gaul, modern-day France; and Mozarabic, from Spain.

Building a Musical Vocabulary: *Gregorian Chant*

Define the following terms as they relate to Gregorian chant:

monophonic texture _____

_____

_____

unmeasured prose rhythm _____

_____

_____

neumes _____

_____

_____

syllabic text setting _____

_____

_____

neumatic text setting _____

_____

_____

melismatic text setting _____

_____

_____

responsorial singing _____

_____

_____

verse _____

_____

_____

respond _____

_____

gradual _____

_____

psalm _____

_____

modes _____

_____

Supplemental Activity: *Identifying Modes*

Insert the name of each of the modes notated below, choosing from the following: Aeolian, Dorian, Ionian, Lydian, Mixolydian, Phrygian.

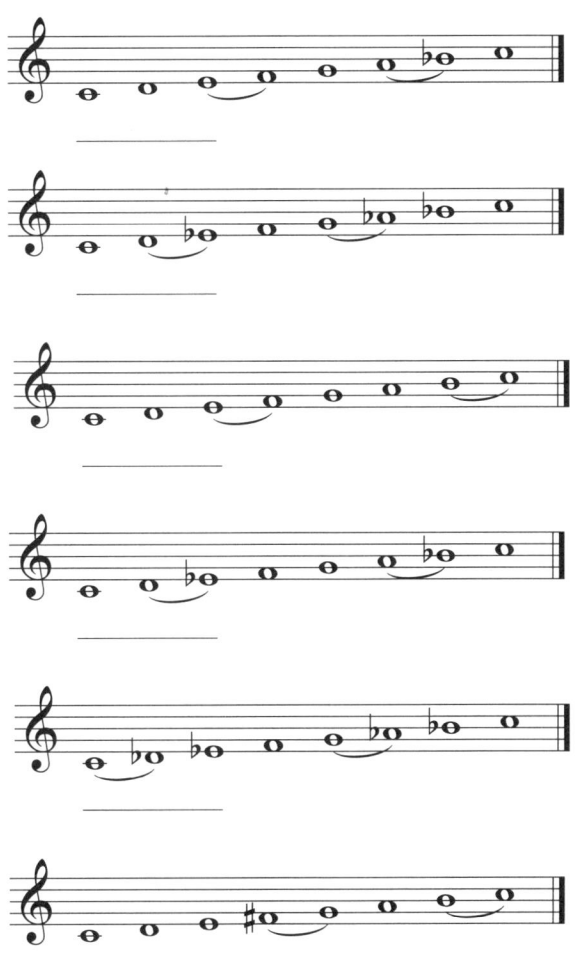

Required Listening: Anonymous, *Haec dies* (Chant)

The chant *Haec dies* is a beautiful example of how music enhanced the most significant service of the Roman Catholic Church—the mass. This chant is drawn from the mass for Easter Sunday. Because Easter is one of the most significant feast days in the church calendar, it is not surprising that the musical setting is quite elaborate.

The prayers that comprise the mass are divided into two categories. The texts that remain unchanged throughout the year are referred to as the Ordinary. The prayers with variable texts appropriate for each day of the church calendar are called the Proper.

What does the designation "anonymous" tell us about the composer of *Haec dies*?

_____

_____

Listen to a recording of the chant *Haec dies*. If possible, follow a score while you listen. Ex. 2.1 shows what the original notation would have looked like. A modern transcription of the same passage is shown in Ex. 2.2.

Ex. 2.1. Anonymous, *Haec dies* (opening), original notation.

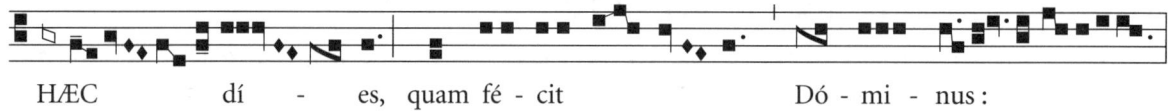

Ex. 2.2. Anonymous, *Haec dies* (opening), modern transcription.

What biblical texts are used in this chant? _____

What is the English translation of the opening line? _____

_____

Circle the correct answer:

On what feast day is this chant performed?
- a) Christmas
- b) Easter
- c) All Saints Day

The texture of this chant can be described as:
- a) monophonic
- b) polyphonic
- c) homophonic

What performance method is used?
a) responsorial
b) antiphonal (alternating choirs)

The predominant text-setting method(s) used are:
a) syllabic
b) neumatic
c) melismatic

This melody is best described as:
a) modal
b) tonal

The rhythm of the chant can be described as:
a) measured
b) unmeasured

Describe the melodic characteristics of *Haec dies* in terms of the following:

1. Range (distance between the highest and the lowest pitches) _____

2. Widest melodic interval _____

3. Most frequently used interval _____

What is the overall musical character of this composition? How is it suited to the specific occasion for which it was intended?

_____
_____
_____
_____
_____
_____

In 1990, an anonymous band named Enigma released a CD entitled *MCMXC a.D.* The "band" was actually Michael Cretu, a Rumanian musician and producer (identified only as "Curly M.C." on the liner notes). This CD featured songs that blended Gregorian chant samples with a sultry female voice and hip hop rhythm tracks. Despite the mystery surrounding its release, the Enigma CD was an instant hit. Cretu's recording project effectively illustrates how old and new material can be blended to create something truly unique.

Exploring Music History: A Guided Approach   Volume 2: Middle Ages to Classical

Hildegard of Bingen

In the late 1990s, some of the best-selling classical CDs were recordings of sacred vocal music written by the 12th-century composer Hildegard of Bingen (1098-1179). The commercial success of these recordings was an unexpected phenomenon—music composed by a nun in the Middle Ages captured the imagination of listeners nearly a thousand years later. Hildegard of Bingen is an even more fascinating figure because of her intriguing and varied career.

Who was Hildegard of Bingen and where did she live?

_____

_____

_____

At what institution was she a religious leader and what was her title?

_____

In what disciplines other than music did she gain respect and success?

_____

_____

Why was this an extraordinary accomplishment for its time?

_____

_____

Name the musical genre for which she is best known. _____

What was the purpose of this genre? _____

_____

_____

What was the texture of her music? _____

How was her music original and innovative? _____

_____

_____

A common practice among Christians in the Middle Ages was "tithing" (donating one-tenth of one's worldly goods to the Church). Hildegard of Bingen was the tenth child in her family and in keeping with this tradition, was offered to the Church by her parents. While accepting a life that demanded contemplation and prayer, Hildegard was still able to develop her many diverse talents and gifts and become a leading figure of her day.

Recommended Listening for Chant:
Anonymous: *Salve regina* (Marian Antiphon)
Anonymous: *Kyrie* (from Mass for Easter Sunday)
Anonymous: *Victimae paschali laudes* (Sequence from Mass for Easter Sunday)
Thomas of Celano: *Dies irae* (Sequence)
Hildegard of Bingen: *Ordo virtutum* (Play of the Virtues)

Note: The works listed above are available in *The Development of Western Music, Anthology and Recordings* (see Appendix A).

Organum

Origins: Early Polyphony

As time went on and groups of church musicians (often monks in monasteries) sang the same chants over periods of months, years, and even generations, it was inevitable that some experimenting would take place. In simple terms, the musicians started "harmonizing." These experiments led to the next significant step in the development of Western music: *polyphony*. Polyphony can be defined as music that simultaneously combines two or more independent lines.

The earliest form of polyphony is called *organum*. When an additional vocal line moves in parallel motion above or below an original chant at the interval of a 4th or 5th, the style is referred to as *parallel organum*.

The parallel organum shown in Ex. 2.3 is drawn from *Musica Enchiriadis*, an anonymous 9th-century treatise that contains the earliest recorded polyphony in Western music. In view of the great importance that the element of harmony acquired, the creation of organum was a significant milestone in the history of Western art music.

Ex. 2.3. Parallel organum from *Musica Enchiriadis* (excerpt).

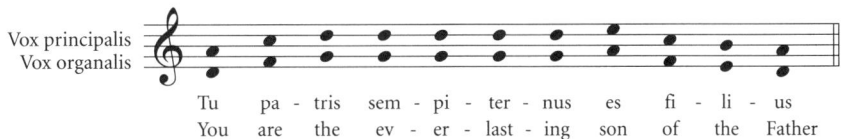

 The development of musical notation paralleled the evolution of polyphony. One notable figure who contributed to this process was an 11th-century monk known to us as Guido of Arezzo (*ca* 991-1050). A particularly interesting innovation developed by Guido was a system for teaching sight singing in which a set of syllables (*ut, re, mi, fa, sol, la*) was used to help singers remember patterns of whole tones and semitones. (If you have used the modern *solfège* system in your musical training, you may recognize these syllables!) Using your search engine, look on the internet for more information about this historically important musician and theorist.

Building a Musical Vocabulary: *Organum*

Define the following terms as they relate to organum:

polyphonic texture _____
_____
_____

organal style _____
_____
_____

discant style _____
_____
_____

cantus firmus _____
_____
_____

rhythmic modes _____
_____
_____

clausula _____
_____
_____

The Notre Dame Cathedral is one of the greatest cathedrals of the Gothic era. Constructed in Paris during the late 12th and early 13th centuries, it has been immortalized in print and film, including Victor Hugo's novel *The Hunchback of Notre Dame*. Use your search engine to look at pictures and read more about the history of this famous church.

Notre Dame School: Léonin and Pérotin

At various times throughout history, artists working in a particular place have forged a common vision that resulted in significant developments and innovations. The use of the word "school" denotes a common style represented by the collective work of such groups of individuals. An early example of a compositional school is the work of the Notre Dame composers in the 12th and 13th centuries.

Two of the leading composers of the Notre Dame School were Léonin and Pérotin. What were their contributions to the development of early polyphony?

Léonin _____

_____

_____

Pérotin _____

_____

_____

Composers of the 12th and 13th centuries often replaced the clausulae in previously composed organum with new ones. Pérotin, for example, composed many substitute clausulae to replace existing ones by Léonin. These independent sections, when removed from their original context, gained a new life and are directly linked to the development of the motet.

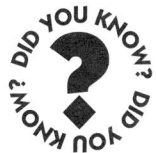

The contemporary vocal ensemble Anonymous IV specializes in medieval music. The group takes its name from the writer of a 13th-century treatise who signed his work using the pen name "Anonymous IV." This mysterious writer was the first to identify Léonin and Pérotin as the leading composers of the Notre Dame School.

Required Listening: Anonymous, *Haec dies* (Organum)

Written in the style of Léonin, this work illustrates how the techniques of the Notre Dame School composers were applied to create polyphonic compositions. The Gregorian chant that you already studied—*Haec dies*—served as the *cantus firmus* and became the structural framework for a new composition.

What was the approximate date of composition for this anonymous work?

_____

Listen to a recording of the organum *Haec dies*. If possible, follow a score while you listen.

Ex. 2.4. Anonymous, *Haec dies* Organum (opening).

How many voices are present in the texture? _____

What term best describes the musical texture? _____

In which voice does the original chant appear? _____

Describe the relationship between the two voices. What are the predominant harmonic intervals? How does the rhythm of the upper voice differ from that of the lower voice?

_____
_____
_____
_____

Historians have often compared the development of polyphony in music with the development of perspective in painting. What parallels do you see in these two developments?

_____
_____
_____

Recommended Listening for Organum:
Léonin: *Alleluia, Pascha nostrum* (organum duplum)
Pérotin: *Mors* (organum quadruplum)

Note: The above examples are available in *The Development of Western Music*, Anthology and Recordings (see Appendix A).

Motet

Origins: 13th-century Motet

When you listened to the organum *Haec dies* you may have noticed that the upper voice had extended melismatic passages. This made the existing text difficult to follow, and the upper voice very awkward to perform. In the 13th century, musicians caught in this situation began adding new texts to the previously textless upper voices of organum. The result was a polytextual composition known as the *motet*.

Motets often combined several languages while mixing sacred and secular content. For example, a Latin chant might have been paired with a French love poem, often suggesting "double meanings" or hidden sub-texts.

The term motet derived from the French word *mot*, meaning "word." Why was this appropriate?

_____
_____
_____

Building a Musical Vocabulary: *13th-century Motet*

Explain the following terms as they relate to the 13th-century motet:

tenor _____

duplum _____

triplum _____

polytextual _____

ostinato _____

Required Listening: Anonymous, *O mitissima/Virgo/Haec dies*

The chant *Haec dies* served yet again as a *cantus firmus* in the 13-century motet *O mitissima/Virgo/Haec dies.* In many respects, this work is typical of the motet as it existed in the 13th century.

Take another look at the unusual title of this composition, and then examine the opening measures of the excerpt in Ex. 2.5. Musicians and historians identify polytextual motets by the opening words of each different text. Why do you think this is a useful practice?

_____

_____

_____

Listen to a recording of *O mitissima/Virgo/Haec dies*. If possible, follow a score while you listen. Answer the questions below:

Ex. 2.5. Anonymous, *O mitissima/Virgo/Haec dies* (opening).

How many voices are present in this texture? _____

What term best describes this musical texture? _____

In which voice is the chant fragment found? How is it treated rhythmically?
_____
_____
_____

Summarize what is expressed in each of the three texts:

triplum _____
_____

duplum _____
_____

tenor _____
_____

Describe the relationship between the upper voices.
_____
_____
_____

What harmonic intervals are prevalent in this work? _____

In the recording you listened to, how were the three voices performed? (Were only voices used, or was an instrument included to double or substitute one or more of the voices?)
_____
_____
_____

14th-century Motet

In the 14th century, the motet remained an important musical genre as it continued to develop and evolve. In keeping with the increasingly secular spirit of the time, the motet frequently incorporated secular texts. Characteristics associated with the 14th-century motet include: active and intricate rhythm; greater variety in harmony; and use of complex polyphonic devices.

Historians use the term *Ars Nova* ("New Art") to designate music from this period. The leading musician from this era was Guillaume de Machaut (*ca* 1300-1377). Machaut was an important composer of both sacred and secular works. You will learn more about his music in Unit Three when we explore secular music in the Middle Ages and Renaissance.

15th-century Motet

With the dawning of the Renaissance era, significant changes in musical style emerged. These changes can be observed in the motet, which became one of the principal forms of sacred music during the 15th century. One of the most significant changes was the use of a single text in place of multiple texts heard simultaneously. This practice grew out of a desire for clarity and direct communication.

Building a Musical Vocabulary: *15th-century Motet*

Define the following terms:

a cappella _____

_____

_____

imitation _____

_____

_____

chordal declamation _____

_____

_____

Franco-Flemish School _____

_____

_____

Josquin des Prez

One of the most significant composers of the Franco-Flemish School was Josquin des Prez (*ca* 1440-1521). Highly acclaimed and hailed as the greatest composer of his generation, he was even compared to the great painter and sculptor Michelangelo. Josquin had a brilliant career, and like many of his contemporaries from the same region, he pursued his profession in Italy. In that country his patrons included the wealthy and powerful Sforza and d'Este families, and he worked in the service of several prestigious churches, including the Sistine Chapel.

Josquin's musical style embodied the humanism of his time. Rich emotional expression and a superb mastery of the contrapuntal style were features that made his music pleasing to the listener, then and now. His output included masses, motets, and secular songs.

Required Listening: Josquin, *Ave Maria...virgo serena*

The motet *Ave Maria...virgo serena* reflects the exalted position given to the Virgin Mary in the Roman Catholic Church during the Renaissance era. A significant number of musical works were written in honor of Mary. Renaissance artists also depicted her frequently in paintings and sculptures, often with the infant Jesus in her arms.

Listen to a recording of *Ave Maria...virgo serena*. If possible, follow a score as you listen. Outline the main characteristics of this composition by answering the questions below:

Ex. 2.6. Josquin, *Ave Maria...virgo serena,* mm. 1-6.

When was this motet composed? _____

How many voices make up this work? _____

What is the language of the text? _____

How is the poem structured? _____

One of the significant features of this motet is the variety of textures present. They include:
- imitation
- pairing of voices
- homophonic (chordal) passages.

For each of the fragments of text given below, identify the type of texture used:

"Ave Maria, gratia plena"   <u>imitation</u>

"Ave cujus conceptio"   _____

"Ave vera virginitas"   _____

"O Mater Dei, memento mei"   _____

Comment briefly on the treatment of the following elements in this motet:

rhythm _____

_____

harmony _____

_____

musical character/mood _____

_____

_____

Based on your study of *Ave Maria...virgo serena*, list five specific traits of Josquin des Prez's musical style:

1. _contrapuntal mastery_____
2. _____
3. _____
4. _____
5. _____

Supplemental Activity: *Comparing a 13th- and 15th-century Motet*

Summarize the similarities and differences between the two motets you have studied by filling in the chart below.

	O mitissima/Virgo/Haec dies	*Ave Maria...virgo serena*
Approximate date		
Identity of composer		
Number of voices		
Sacred or secular		
Polytextual or single text		
Use of cantus firmus		
Harmonic language		
Use of imitation		

Exploring Music History: A Guided Approach   Volume 2: Middle Ages to Classical

Which of these motets did you enjoy listening to more, and why?

_____

_____

_____

Recommended Listening for Motet:
Guillaume de Machaut: *Hareu! Hareu! le feu/Helas!/Obediens*
Guillaume Dufay: *Alma redemptoris mater*
Roland de Lassus: *Tristis est anima mea*

Mass

The mass is the most important service in the liturgy of the Roman Catholic Church. It includes prayers, readings from the bible, and a re-enactment of the Last Supper, referred to as the Eucharist, or Holy Communion.

In the Middle Ages, the earliest mass settings took the form of monophonic chants, as we have already seen in the *Haec dies* from the Gregorian Mass for Easter Sunday. As the art of polyphony flowered in the 12th and 13th centuries, many chants—particularly those from the Mass Proper—served as the basis for organum. The first complete polyphonic setting of the Mass Ordinary was composed in the 14th century by Guillaume de Machaut. Machaut's *Messe de Nostre Dame* is thought to be the longest extant work from the Middle Ages.

In the Renaissance era, composers used complete mass settings to demonstrate their mastery of the contrapuntal devices from the time. The mass, consisting of polyphonic settings of the five movements of the ordinary, became a favored and important musical genre.

Building a Musical Vocabulary: *Mass*

Name the two categories of prayers in the mass:

_____   _____

Fill in the appropriate term for each type of prayer described below:

_____ The prayers with texts that remain the same throughout the year.

_____ The prayers with texts that change depending on the church calendar.

List the five prayers of the Mass Ordinary:

_____

_____

_____

_____

_____

List four of the prayers of the Mass Proper:

_____

_____

_____

_____

> Over time, the mass moved from the church to the concert hall as it evolved from functional liturgical music to a prominent musical genre. Throughout this transition, the words of the Mass Ordinary remained constant. Composers from all eras, including Bach, Mozart, Beethoven, and Schubert, wrote masses that incorporated the stylistic currents of their time.

The Reformation and Counter-Reformation

During the 16th century, a series of significant events led to a shift in the position of dominance held by the Roman Catholic Church. These historic changes affected the traditions of sacred music, including the mass.

Explain the importance of the following individuals and events as they relate to music during the Renaissance:

Martin Luther (1483-1546) _____

_____

_____

_____

Protestant Reformation _____

_____

_____

_____

Counter-Reformation _____

_____

_____

_____

Council of Trent (1545-1563) _____

_____

_____

_____

Giovanni Pierluigi da Palestrina

The music of Giovanni Pierluigi da Palestrina (*ca* 1525-1594) is associated with the Roman Catholic Counter-Reformation. A deeply religious man, Palestrina expressed his faith through his musical style. His sacred music embodied the ideals of church leaders who sought to restore reverent attitudes to liturgical music.

Required Listening: Palestrina, "Gloria" from *Pope Marcellus Mass*

The *Pope Marcellus Mass (Missa Papae Marcelli)* is a polyphonic setting of the five movements of the Ordinary. It is freely composed, not based on any pre-existing material, and is intended to be sung *a cappella*.

Listen to a recording of the "Gloria" from *Pope Marcellus Mass*. If possible, follow a score as you listen. Answer the questions below.

Ex. 2.7. Palestrina, "Gloria" from *Pope Marcellus Mass,* mm. 1-8.

When was this work published? _____

What is the language of the text? _____

How many voices are employed? _____

What is the texture of the opening line "Gloria in excelsis Deo"? _____

As was the case with Josquin's *Ave Maria… virgo serena*, the texture changes frequently in this work, and the number of voices heard at any one time changes from phrase to phrase. This is one way in which clarity of text is achieved.

Suggest two other features that make the text easy to understand.

1. _____

2. _____

Why is this a desirable characteristic in this composition?

_____

_____

_____

Having listened to a recording of this work, comment on the mood and character created.

_____

_____

_____

Based on your study of the "Gloria" from *Pope Marcellus Mass,* list five specific traits of Palestrina's musical style:

1. _clarity in text setting_____

2. _____

3. _____

4. _____

5. _____

Although Palestrina is best known for his finely crafted sacred music, he also wrote approximately one hundred secular madrigals (songs) early in his career. He later apologized for these works, and "blushed and grieved" at having written such music.

Recommended Listening for Mass:
Guillaume de Machaut: *Messe de Nostre Dame*
Guillaume Dufay: *Missa L'homme armé*
Josquin des Prez: *Missa La sol fa ré mi*
Palestrina: *Missa Lauda Sion*

Review and Reflection

The four types of sacred vocal music you have studied in this unit are strikingly different from one another. Each represents a particular stage in the evolution and development of Western art music.

Compare and contrast the four genres by filling in the chart below:

	Gregorian chant	Organum	Motet	Mass
Texture	monophonic	polyphonic		
Origins				
Formal structure				
Composers/ schools				
Composition titles				

For the average churchgoer in the Middle Ages and Renaissance, attending mass was a mystical experience that was heightened by the music. Most of the members of the congregation did not speak or understand Latin, the language in which the majority of prayers were sung or chanted. Imagine yourself in this position. What effect would this have on you?

_____

_____

_____

Quiz

1. Match each item on the left to one of the descriptions on the right:

   polyphonic   _____   a. one note sung per syllable

   cantus firmus   _____   b. vocal music performed without instruments

   syllabic   _____   c. a single line of melody

   a cappella   _____   d. 2-4 notes sung per syllable

   responsorial   _____   e. many notes sung to one syllable

   monophonic   _____   f. a borrowed melody often heard in the tenor

   neumatic   _____   g. two or more lines sounding together

   melismatic   _____   h. alternating between solo voice and chorus

2. Name two composers of the Notre Dame School.

   _____   _____

3. Name five significant style features for each of the following composers:

   Josquin des Prez

   _____

   _____

   _____

   _____

   Palestrina

   _____

   _____

   _____

   _____

UNIT THREE

SECULAR VOCAL MUSIC OF THE MIDDLE AGES AND RENAISSANCE

Timeline

A.D. 476	850	1150	1300	1450	1600
		MIDDLE AGES		**RENAISSANCE**	
Dark Ages		Gothic			
		Romanesque	Ars Nova		
GENRES					
		Chanson ·			
				Madrigal · · · · · ·	
COMPOSERS					
"Anonymous" ·					
		Troubadours and Trouvères		Italian Madrigalists	
		Moniot d'Arras	Guillaume de Machaut		
				Carlo Gesualdo	
				English Madrigalists	

Until now, our exploration of medieval and Renaissance music has focused only on sacred music. However, music making outside of the Church was also an integral part of medieval life.

It is unfortunate that secular music of the Middle Ages was not preserved to the same degree as sacred music. Church musicians saw themselves as the custodians of a rich and ever-growing music tradition. For them, recording music in manuscript form was one way of ensuring that it would be preserved for future generations. For secular musicians, however, documenting the music in print was not a priority. As a result, our first-hand sources for secular music are more limited in number. Further, because notation was still in its infancy, many questions arise about performance practices for the secular manuscripts that do survive.

In vocal music, the two most important secular genres during the Middle Ages and Renaissance eras were the *chanson* and the *madrigal*. The *chanson* flourished in French-speaking regions in the Middle Ages and Renaissance, while the madrigal developed first in 16th-century Italy and later in Elizabethan England.

Chanson

The French term *chanson* simply means "song." In the 12th and 13th centuries, aristocratic poet-musicians known as *troubadours* and *trouvères* composed songs consisting of monophonic melodies. In many cases only the poems were documented; when the music was notated, only the pitches were written down because rhythmic notation was not yet standardized. Evidence also suggests that in the Middle Ages, instrumental accompaniments were improvised to enhance the single-line melodies. In re-creating this repertoire today, many aspects of performance such as rhythm, meter, and use of instruments are based on a combination of research and conjecture.

Building a Musical Vocabulary: *Chanson*

Define and explain the role of each of the following as they relate to the development of secular music:

goliards _____

_____

jongleurs _____

_____

By what name were female *jongleurs* known? _____

troubadours _____

_____

_____

trouvères _____

_____

By what name were the German counterparts to *troubadours* and *trouvères* known?

_____

strophic form _____

_____

_____

psaltery _____

_____

_____

dulcimer _____

_____

_____

vielle _____

_____

_____

 Music scholars often turn to the visual arts for information about the performance of music and the use of instruments. This type of research is known as *iconography*. For scholars interested in secular music of the Middle Ages and Renaissance, iconography is especially important because there are so few music manuscripts. In your search engine, use the phrase "iconography and music" to view artwork and learn more about the depiction of music by artists.

Required Listening: Moniot d'Arras, *Ce fut en mai*

This charming courtly *trouvère* song offers us a glimpse into medieval society. Although it was composed almost one thousand years ago, the subject matter of this chanson is timeless; the sentiment expressed is similar to that of many songs written today.

Who was Moniot d'Arras?

_____

_____

_____

Listen to a recording of *Ce fut en mai.* If possible, follow a score as you listen. Answer the questions below:

Ex. 3.1. Moniot d'Arras, *Ce fut en mai* (opening phrase).

Approximate date of composition _____

Texture _____ Language of text _____

Translation of title _____

Summarize the story that is recounted in this poem.

_____

_____

_____

_____

The setting of this song is strophic. How many verses are there? _____

Which of the following correctly shows the internal structure of each verse?
- a) aabb
- b) abcb
- b) abba

What is the rhyme scheme? _____

Referring to your score or the excerpt in Ex. 3.1, describe the melody by commenting on the following:

The range (distance between the highest and lowest notes).

_____

The use of alternate endings. (How do they differ from each other?)

_____

How closely does the music mirror the words in this song? _____

Describe the performance that you listened to by answering the following questions:

What instruments were used? _____

_____

What role do the instruments play in enhancing the overall effect?

_____

_____

Among the more famous medieval troubadours and trouvères are Raimbaut de Vaqueiras, Guiraut de Bornelh, Adam de la Halle, and Richard the Lion Hearted. Search the internet for information about these celebrated figures. Be on the look out for websites that offer sound-clips of *chansons* written by these poet-musicians.

The 14th-century Ars Nova

By the 14th century, the development of musical notation had advanced significantly. The evolution of polyphony in both sacred and secular genres was spurred on by the perfection of a precise rhythmic notation, coupled with pitch notation.

In a now famous treatise called *Ars Nova*, the 14th-century composer Philippe de Vitry advocated the acceptance of many rhythmic innovations, including a duple subdivision of the beat. Seven centuries later, we still use de Vitry's title, *Ars Nova*, to refer to the music and art of his time. While the *Ars Nova* represents a high point in the development of music in the Middle Ages, it also foreshadowed many changes to come in the Renaissance.

Translate the term *Ars Nova*. _____

What term did de Vitry use to denote the musical practice of the previous century?
_____

The musical developments in the *Ars Nova* extended to the *chanson*, which became a sophisticated courtly song in the 14th century. In terms of formal structure, the vocal music of this period often derived its shape from the poetry itself; whatever form the poem took might be clearly reflected in the construction of the music.

Name three fixed forms of French poetry popular in the *Ars Nova*.

1. _____ 2. _____ 3. _____

Explain the construction of the *rondeau*. _____
_____
_____
_____

Guillaume de Machaut

One of the most celebrated figures of the 14th century was Guillaume de Machaut (*ca* 1300-1377). Known in his time as both a poet and a musician, he stands out in the history of music as the single most important composer in the Middle Ages. Today Machaut's music is regarded as the finest example of the *Ars Nova* tradition.

Briefly summarize Machaut's rich and varied career.

_____
_____
_____
_____

Name some of the musical genres developed by Machaut.

_____

_____

_____

 A famous example of Machaut's contrapuntal ingenuity is his work *Ma fin est mon commencement*. The title, which means "My Ending is My Beginning," hints at the complex overall design of this three-voice work. For example, the melody of the middle voice is the same as the upper voice written backwards. At the same time, the bottom voice contains a melody that, half way through the song, continues in retrograde (backwards). This type of hidden design appealed to *Ars Nova* composers and remains fascinating to 21st-century observers.

Required Listening: Machaut, *Puis qu'en oubli*

Listen to a recording of *Puis qu'en oubli*. If possible, follow a score while you listen. Answer the questions below:

Ex. 3.2. Machaut, *Puis qu'en oubli* (opening phrase).

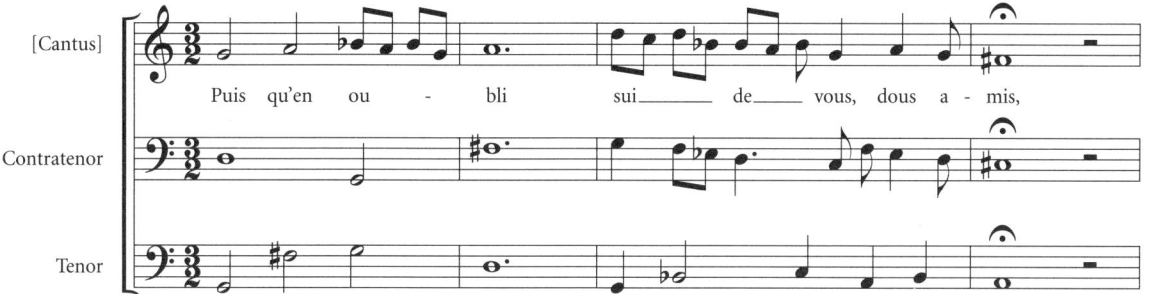

Approximate date of composition _____

Language of text _____

Translation of title _____

Texture _____ Number of voices _____

Musical/poetic form _____ (A-B-a-A-a-b-A-B)

What is the song about? _____

_____

_____

Was this composition based on a *cantus firmus*, or were all of the parts newly composed?

_____

In the recording you listened to, were all of the parts sung? Did instruments double or replace any of the voices? If so, describe what instruments were used.

_____
_____
_____

Describe the music by commenting on the following features:

Text setting _____
_____

Relationship of the voices (Are they distinct? Do the parts ever cross?)
_____
_____
_____

Harmonic language/intervals used _____
_____
_____

Explain why so much musical repetition takes place. _____
_____
_____

Rhythm _____
_____

Based on your study of *Puis qu'en oubli,* list five specific traits of Machaut's musical style:

1. _____
2. _____
3. _____
4. _____
5. _____

Recommended Listening for Chanson:
Raimbaut de Vaqueiras: *Kalenda maya*
Guiraut de Bornelh: *Reis glorios*
Adam de la Halle: *Robin m'Aime* from *Jeu de Robin et Marion*
Guillaume de Machaut: *Rose, liz*
Johannes Ockeghem: *L'autre d'antan*
Roland de Lassus: *Bon jour mon coeur*
Clément Jannequin: *Les cris de Paris*

Madrigal

The most distinctive secular vocal genre of the late Renaissance was the madrigal. Initially it flourished in the small aristocratic courts of Italy. By the end of the 16th century, the madrigal had been introduced in Elizabethan England, where the genre enjoyed immense popularity. An intimate relationship between poetry and music was a characteristic feature of the madrigal.

Building a Musical Vocabulary: *Madrigal*

Define the following terms:

madrigal _____

_____

_____

word painting _____

_____

_____

chromaticism _____

_____

_____

nonsense syllables _____

_____

_____

countertenor _____

_____

_____

Italian Madrigal

The evolution of the Italian madrigal involves three phases of development. Outline briefly the characteristics of the genre during each of these phases:

ca 1525-1550 _____
_____
_____

ca 1550-1580 _____
_____
_____

ca 1580-1620 _____
_____
_____

Name four prominent Italian madrigalists:

1. _____ 3. _____

2. _____ 4. _____

What topics were popular in madrigal texts? _____
_____
_____

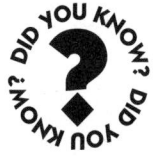

The term *madrigal* was also used in 14th-century Italy in reference to both poetic and musical works. These early madrigals were most often strophic, and did not display the use of word painting and intimate relationship of text and music that are typical of their 16th-century counterparts. One example of these early madrigals is *Fenice fu'* by Jacopo da Bologna (*fl.* 1340-1360).

Required Listening: Carlo Gesualdo, *Moro lasso, al mio duolo*

This late-Renaissance Italian work exemplifies the degree of complexity and refinement that the madrigal attained as it evolved and developed. The composer of this madrigal was Carlo Gesualdo (*ca* 1561-1613). His "mannered" use of extreme chromaticism and word painting is representative of the late Renaissance style.

Listen to a recording of *Moro lasso, al mio duolo*. If possible, follow a score while you listen. Answer the questions below:

Ex. 3.3. Gesualdo, *Moro lasso, al mio duolo,* mm. 1-6.

Approximate date of composition _____

Language _____

Translation of title _____

Number of voices _____ Texture _____

In the recording you listened to, was this madrigal performed with instruments, or *a cappella*? _____

Summarize what the poem is about. _____
_____
_____
_____

How is the poetic content of this madrigal related to Gesualdo's personal life?
(**Hint:** Look up Carlo Gesauldo on the internet or in a textbook to find information on his personal life.)
_____
_____
_____
_____

Comment on each of the following musical elements:

text setting _____
_____

degree of virtuosity _____
_____

Exploring Music History: A Guided Approach   Volume 2: Middle Ages to Classical

harmony _____
_____
_____

The previous music example and the next excerpt contain word painting. For both examples, translate the text into English and explain how the technique of word painting has been utilized.

Translation of "Moro lasso, al mio duolo" (from Ex. 3.3) _____
_____

Word painting _____
_____

Ex. 3.4. Gesualdo, *Moro lasso, al mio duolo,* mm. 3-7.

Translation of "Chi mi puo dar vita" (from Ex. 3.4) _____
_____

Word painting _____
_____

Find one additional example of word painting in *Moro lasso, al mio duolo.*

Italian text _____

Translation of text _____

Word painting _____
_____

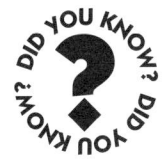
Women played a prominent role in the performance of Renaissance madrigal repertoire. One of the most famous ensembles in 16th-century Italy was the "Concerto delle donne" (Ensemble of the Ladies). This group consisted of four aristocratic amateur singers. Their exceptional artistry and virtuosity garnered them the praise of contemporary audiences and inspired leading composers of the day to create new works for them.

English Madrigal

By the 1580s, the popularity of the madrigal had spread from Italy to England. The genre found fertile ground in the court of Elizabeth I, who reigned from 1558-1603. Elizabeth possessed discriminating musical taste and during her reign, the madrigal grew and developed considerably. The publication of *Musica transalpina* in 1588 launched the popularity of the madrigal in England.

What does the title *Musica transalpina* mean in English? _____

_____

Explain what was contained in this publication. _____

_____

_____

In embracing the madrigal, the English incorporated certain features that made it stand apart from its Italian counterpart. What elements and devices did English composers like to include in their madrigals?

_____

_____

_____

Name four English madrigalists.

1. _____   3. _____

2. _____   4. _____

In 1601, a famous collection of twenty-five English madrigals entitled *The Triumphes of Oriana* was published. England's leading madrigalists composed these works in honor of Queen Elizabeth I. Each madrigal concludes with the same couplet: "Then sang the shepherds and nymphs of Diana, Long live fair Oriana." During this era, mythological figures were frequently used to represent or honor royalty. Oriana would have represented Elizabeth.

Required Listening: Farmer, *Fair Phyllis I Saw Sitting All Alone*

Who was John Farmer? _____
_____

Listen to a recording of *Fair Phyllis*. If possible, follow a score while you listen. Answer the following questions:

Approximate date of composition _____

Number of voices _____

Texture _____

What is the poem about? _____
_____
_____
_____
_____

Comment on the following musical elements:

meter/rhythm _____
_____
_____

text setting _____
_____
_____

use of imitation _____
_____
_____

The next four excerpts all contain word painting. For each example, explain how the technique of word painting has been utilized.

Ex. 3.5. Farmer, *Fair Phyllis*, mm. 1-4.

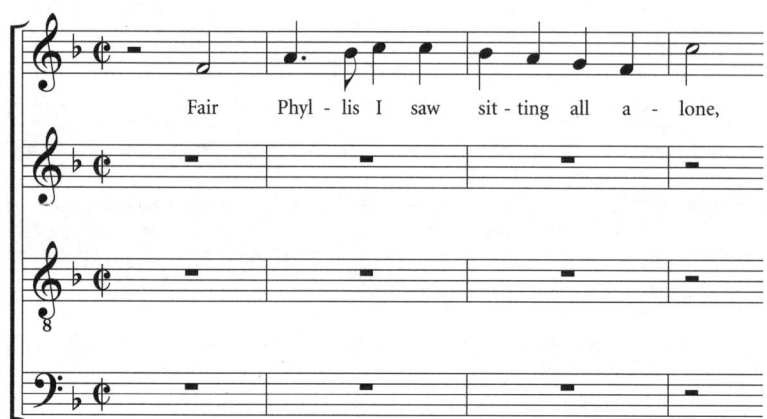

Word painting for "Fair Phyllis I saw sitting all alone" (Ex. 3.5):

_____

_____

Ex. 3.6. Farmer, *Fair Phyllis*, mm. 4-7.

Word painting for "Feeding her flock" (Ex. 3.6):

_____

_____

Ex. 3.7. Farmer, *Fair Phyllis,* mm. 18 and 19.

Word painting for "Up and down" (Ex. 3.7):

_____

_____

Ex. 3.8. Farmer, *Fair Phyllis,* mm. 35-38.

Word painting for "fell a-kissing" (Ex. 3.8):

_____

_____

Recommended Listening for Madrigal:
Jacob Arcadelt: *Il bianco cigno*
Luca Marenzio: *Cantate ninfe*
Claudio Monteverdi: *Ohimè! Se tanto amate*
Claudio Monteverdi: *A un giro sol*
Orlando Gibbons: *The Silver Swan*
Thomas Weelkes: *As Vesta was descending*
Thomas Morley: *My Bonnie Lass She Smileth*

 Peter Schickele, renowned American musicologist and humorist (also known as PDQ Bach), created a delightful parody of English madrigals entitled *The Triumphs of Thusnelda,* which includes *My Bonnie Lass She Smelleth*. This "madrigal" combines Renaissance polyphony and word painting with English nonsense syllables and 20th-century scat singing. Old and new fans of PDQ Bach can find this music on *The Dreaded PDQ Bach Collection* (Vanguard 159/62).

Supplemental Activity: *Learning About Elizabeth I*

Queen Elizabeth I and the era in which she lived continue to fascinate us today, and filmmakers past and present have been attracted to this compelling figure. To place your study of the music from this period in a broader cultural context, you may enjoy viewing some of these films:

The Private Lives of Elizabeth and Essex
Shakespeare in Love
Elizabeth
Elizabeth R (BBC Mini-series)

Review and Reflection

Now that you have completed your study of both sacred and secular vocal music of the Middle Ages and Renaissance, complete the chart below to summarize your understanding of the music from both eras.

	Middle Ages	**Renaissance**
Major genres	_____	_____
	_____	_____
	_____	_____
	_____	_____
Composers	_____	_____
	_____	_____
	_____	_____
	_____	_____
	_____	_____
Techniques and devices	cantus firmus	word painting
	_____	_____
	_____	_____
	_____	_____

Of the works you studied in this unit, which did you enjoy the most and why?

_____
_____
_____

Exploring Music History: A Guided Approach — Volume 2: Middle Ages to Classical

Quiz

1. Choosing from the works you have studied in this unit, give the title that best applies to each of the descriptions below:

   A 13th-century trouvère song. _____

   A late-Renaissance Italian madrigal. _____

   A 14th-century chanson for three voices. _____

   An English work demonstrating word painting. _____

   A work composed in the Ars Nova style. _____

   A monophonic song in strophic form. _____

   An early 17th-century work demonstrating
     extreme chromaticism. _____

   An Elizabethan madrigal with a pastoral text. _____

   A polyphonic work whose text exhibits
     a rondeau form. _____

   A monophonic song with French text. _____

2. List two specific musical style traits for each composer below.

   Guillaume de Machaut _____

   _____

   John Farmer _____

   _____

   Moniot d'Arras _____

   _____

   Carlo Gesualdo _____

   _____

3. What did *Musica transalpina* contain, and what was its significance?

   _____

   _____

UNIT FOUR

VOCAL MUSIC OF THE BAROQUE AND CLASSICAL ERAS

Timeline

1600		1750	1825
BAROQUE		**CLASSICAL**	
GENRES			
Opera ···			
Cantata ··	···		
Oratorio ···	···		
COMPOSERS			
Florentine Camerata			
Claudio Monteverdi		Christoph Wilibald Gluck	
Henry Purcell		Franz Joseph Haydn	
Johann Sebastian Bach		Wolfgang Amadeus Mozart	

Opera

Origins: Florentine Camerata

Unlike any other musical era, the dawning of the Baroque period is defined by the birth of a remarkable new genre—opera. The first operas were written in the early 1600s in Florence, Italy, where a group of intellectuals, artists, and composers attempted to recreate the performance style of ancient Greek drama. This group became known as the Florentine Camerata. Four hundred years later, opera continues to captivate audiences throughout the world.

Name four members of the Florentine Camerata:

_____   _____

_____   _____

Name two operas composed by members of this group:

Title _____ Composer _____

Title _____ Composer _____

The Florentine Camerata developed *monody*, a musical texture that consisted of a vocal melody unfolding over a bass line supported by a simple chordal accompaniment, as in Ex. 4.1. Monody allowed the solo singer to deliver the text with clarity and emotional intensity. This emphasis on the outermost voices (soprano and bass) was in marked contrast to the dense polyphony of the 16th century and became one of the principal characteristics of the emerging Baroque style. Examples and descriptions of this new texture were contained in a 1602 publication entitled *Le Nuove Musiche* ("The New Music") by Florentine composer Giulio Caccini. The example below is drawn from this source.

Ex. 4.1. Caccini, *Amarilli mia bella,* mm. 1-7.

 The oldest surviving opera from the work of the Florentine Camerata is *Euridice* by Peri and Caccini. In light of the general interest in Greek culture during the late 16th century, it is not surprising that the plots chosen for the earliest operas were drawn from Greek mythology. If you are not already familiar with the story of Orpheus and Euridice, you may wish to learn more about it by exploring the internet. Search on the phrase "Orpheus myth in opera."

While opera began as an elite art form and initially flourished in the palaces of the Italian nobility, it soon captured the attention of a wider audience. In 1637, the very first public opera house opened in Venice. A building frenzy ensued, and in the decades that followed, opera houses were constructed throughout Italy, and later throughout Europe.

Name two European opera houses built in the 17th century and the cities in which they were located:

  Opera house _____ City _____

  Opera house _____ City _____

Name two renowned 20th-century opera houses and the cities in which they are located:

  Opera house _____ City _____

  Opera house _____ City _____

 Using your search engine, look up some of the following opera houses: La Fenice, La Scala, Teatro de Liceu, Sydney Opera House, Drottningholm Court Theatre, Metropolitan Opera, Covent Garden, Bayreuth Festspieltheater. What similarities and differences do you observe in their architecture and design? If you could visit one, which would you choose, and why?

Building a Musical Vocabulary: *Opera*

Explain each of the following as they relate to opera in the Baroque era:

monody _____
_____

stile rappresentativo _____
_____

libretto _____
_____

aria _____
_____

da capo aria _____
_____

chorus _____
_____

stile concitato _____
_____

ground bass _____
_____

sinfonia _____
_____

ritornello _____
_____

recitativo secco _____

_____

_____

recitativo accompagnato _____

_____

_____

opera seria _____

_____

_____

castrato _____

_____

_____

Name two famous castrati from the Baroque era:

_____   _____

Claudio Monteverdi

Historians regard Claudio Monteverdi (1567-1643) as one of the principal composers whose style and output paralleled the transition from the Renaissance to the Baroque era. Building on the foundation established through the work of the Florentine Camerata, Monteverdi elevated opera to its full artistic potential. He was so committed to projecting the meaning of the words with sincerity and intensity that his motto was, "the text is the master, the music the servant." In his music we find an emotional passion remarkable for its time.

In which Italian courts was Monteverdi active and how long was his tenure in each?

_____

_____

_____

_____

In 1613, Monteverdi was appointed choirmaster to St. Mark's Basilica, an appointment he kept for the remainder of his life. In which city is this famous church located?

_____

 St. Mark's Basilica, unlike most cathedrals of its time, has two opposing choir lofts, each containing an organ. (Normally there is a single organ located at the rear of the building.) This aspect of the church's architecture enabled composers to experiment with special effects and polychoral techniques. Works such as *Symphoniae Sacrae* by Venetian composer Giovanni Gabrieli exemplify this polychoral style.

Comment on Monteverdi's contributions to each of the following genres:

sacred vocal music _____

_____

_____

madrigal _____

_____

_____

Name the operas by Monteverdi that were first performed in each of the following years:

1607 _____

1608 _____

1640 _____

1642 _____

Required Listening: Monteverdi, *The Coronation of Poppea* (Coronation Scene)

Monteverdi composed *The Coronation of Poppea* (*L'Incoronazione di Poppea*) at the end of his career. By this time, public opera houses had been established in major Italian cities. Works composed for these venues were intended to appeal to a wider audience, and Monteverdi's choice of plot for this opera demonstrates this trend. *The Coronation of Poppea* includes characters drawn from all social classes depicted with their human frailties.

Listen to a recording or watch a video performance of Act 3, Scene 7 (Coronation Scene) from *The Coronation of Poppea*. If possible follow a score. Answer the questions below and complete the listening outline for the Coronation Scene:

Year of its premiere _____

Librettist _____ Type of opera _____

Exploring Music History: A Guided Approach Volume 2: Middle Ages to Classical

Describe the principal characters and identify their voice types:

Character	Voice type	Brief description
Nero	castrato	Emperor of Rome
Poppea		
Seneca		
Ottavia		
Ottone		
Drusilla		

Unlike most of the operas created in the first forty years of the 17th century, this work was not based on mythology. On what was this story based?

_____
_____
_____

Like many of the stage works of this era, this opera begins with a Prologue. We are introduced to Fortuna (Fortune), Virtu (Virtue), and Amore (Love) as they argue about which of them has the most influence. Amore proclaims himself the winner, since his fickle nature has the power to shape the destiny of mankind. This sets the stage for the drama that follows.

Summarize the plot of this three-act opera.

_____
_____
_____
_____
_____
_____

How did Monteverdi make use each of the following elements in *The Coronation of Poppea*?

aria _____
_____
_____

recitative _____
_____
_____

chorus _____
_____
_____

duet _____
_____
_____

ritornello _____
_____
_____

sinfonia _____
_____
_____

Coronation Scene (Act 3, Scene 7)

This scene opens festively with the Chorus of Consuls and Tribunes. What sentiments are being expressed and how does Monteverdi capture these emotions?

_____
_____
_____
_____

Comment briefly on each of the following musical elements in this chorus:

texture _____

meter _____

text setting _____

word painting _____
_____

The chorus is followed by a short instrumental sinfonia that allows for the departure of all the characters. Only Nero and Poppea remain on the stage to share an intimate moment. Despite the sordid events that have led up to Poppea's coronation, the duet sung by these characters is one of the most exquisite and moving examples of Monteverdi's art.

Exploring Music History: A Guided Approach — Volume 2: Middle Ages to Classical

Duet: "Pur ti miro"

Ex. 4.2. Monteverdi, "Pur ti miro" from *The Coronation of Poppea*, mm. 344-347.

What are the two characters expressing?
_____
_____

How does the texture employed by Monteverdi mirror this exchange?
_____
_____

What is the formal structure of this duet?
_____

Within Section A, a ground bass is used. Explain this device and how it is used here.
_____
_____
_____
_____

On the staff below, write the melodic line that is repeated as the ground bass:

How is contrast achieved within Section B?
_____
_____
_____

When Section B is repeated, how do the performers vary this material?

_____

_____

On the recording you listened to, what instruments were used to support the voices?

_____

Based on your study of *The Coronation of Poppea*, list five specific traits of Monteverdi's musical style:

1. _____
2. _____
3. _____
4. _____
5. _____

Henry Purcell

In his brief but illustrious career, Henry Purcell (1659-1695) served four different British monarchs. During this patronage, Purcell produced a large body of music that included operas, dramatic music, sacred and secular vocal works, keyboard music, and instrumental works. Historians often refer to Purcell as the "British Orpheus" because of the compelling lyricism of his compositions.

Required Listening: Purcell, *Dido and Aeneas* (Final Scene)

Despite its relatively short length and humble origins as a work intended for a performance by the students of a school for girls, *Dido and Aeneas* stands out as the first great English opera. Building on the story of ill-fated lovers depicted in Virgil's *Aeneid,* the opera fuses together the dynamic string writing of the Italian tradition, the regal character of the French overture, and the lyricism of the English vocal style.

Listen to a recording of the Final Scene in Act 3 of *Dido and Aeneas*. If possible, follow a score while you listen. Answer the questions below and complete the listening outline for the Final Scene:

In what year was *Dido and Aeneas* first performed? _____

Librettist _____ Type of opera <u>English opera</u>

Source of plot _____

Exploring Music History: A Guided Approach   Volume 2: Middle Ages to Classical

Describe the principal characters and identify their voice types:

Character	Voice type	Brief description
Dido	soprano	Queen of Carthage
Aeneas	_____	_____
Belinda	_____	_____
Sorceress	_____	_____

What other characters (groups or individuals) appear throughout the opera?
_____
_____

Summarize the plot of this three-act opera.
_____
_____
_____
_____
_____

Act 3, Final Scene: *Dido's Lament*
Recitative: "Thy hand, Belinda"

Ex. 4.3. Purcell, "Thy hand, Belinda," from *Dido and Aeneas,* mm. 1-5.

Which of the following correctly describes the type of recitative shown in Ex. 4.3?
  a) *recitativo secco* (accompanied by continuo only)
  b) *recitative accompagnato* (instrumental ensemble)

Explain how word painting is employed in the musical setting of each of the following words:

"darkness" _____
_____

"death" _____
_____

Aria: "When I am laid in earth"

Meter _____   Key _____

Ex. 4.4. Purcell, "When I am laid in earth," from *Dido and Aeneas* mm. 1-11.

The bass line for this aria is built from a repeated melodic passage.

What is the name for this device? _____

How many times is this bass line repeated? _____

How does the descending chromatic bass line reflect the meaning of the text?

_____

_____

_____

Describe the musical setting of the following:

"laid in earth" _____

_____

"remember me" _____

_____

Chorus: "With drooping wings"

Which characters sing this chorus? _____

Why do you think Purcell followed Dido's dramatic lament with this chorus?

_____

_____

_____

_____

Describe the musical setting of the following:

"with drooping wings" _____

_____

"soft" _____

_____

Based on your study of *Dido and Aeneas*, list five specific traits of Purcell's musical style:

1. use of dance rhythms throughout the opera
2.
3.
4.
5.

Handel and Italian Opera in England

After the construction of the first public opera houses in Italy in the early 17th century, *opera seria* spread throughout Europe, enjoying great popularity in many cities. The works of George Frideric Handel (1685-1759) represent an important stage in the development of Baroque opera. During his years in Hamburg, Italy, and Hanover, he learned and perfected his craft.

Handel's rise to fame coincided with his arrival in London. His first opera for the London stage, *Rinaldo* (1711), captured the public's interest and launched a spectacular career for the German-born composer. Over the next thirty years, Handel dominated the London opera scene. During that time he created about forty operas, several of which are still performed today (*Giulio Cesare, Xerxes, Orlando*, and *Alcina*). While he championed Italian opera, Handel also incorporated aspects of French, German, and English style into the genre.

 Handel not only composed Italian operas, but he also produced, directed, and publicized their performances. His legendary temper is well documented in vivid accounts of disputes with less than co-operative singers. One such occurrence was an incident in which the famous soprano Francesca Cuzzoni, after refusing to sing an aria as written, was allegedly lifted and all but thrown through a window by Handel!

Gluck and Operatic Reform

German-born composer Christoph Willibald Gluck (1714-1787) occupies an important place in the history of opera because of the reforms he introduced. By the late Baroque era, operas had begun to favor empty musical display over dramatic integrity. The overtures often had little to do with the work that followed, lengthy ballets were a distraction, and the stars of the day—the singers—would often substitute an aria from a different opera if they felt it would display their virtuosity more effectively.

Gluck's primary goal was to restore dramatic integrity to opera. As a composer of *opera seria* during the 18th century, he adhered to the long-standing practice of looking to mythology for operatic plots, which had been the practice of Handel and his contemporaries. Because his long and fruitful career took him to major cultural centers such as Prague, Rome, London, Vienna, and Paris, Gluck also brought a cosmopolitan outlook to his work. Unlike many of his contemporaries, he was willing to fuse together many national influences into a unique and revitalized operatic style. These influences included the vigorous instrumental writing of the Italian and German schools, and the sublime choral traditions of the French. These international elements, along with an increased use of accompanied recitative, imparted a noble simplicity and graceful majesty to his works.

What specific reforms did Gluck introduce into his operas?

_____

_____

_____

Name four operas by Gluck:

1. _____   3. _____

2. _____   4. _____

Gluck was the music instructor of Princess Maria Antonia of Austria, daughter of Empress Maria Theresa. Later, as the Queen of France, Marie Antoinette (her French name) continued to admire and publicly support Gluck's music.

Building a Musical Vocabulary: *Classical Opera*

Explain the following terms:

opera buffa _____

_____

_____

Singspiel _____

_____

_____

"trouser role" _____

_____

_____

overture _____

_____

_____

modified Sonata-Allegro form _____
_____
_____

terzetto _____
_____
_____

Wolfgang Amadeus Mozart

Wolfgang Amadeus Mozart (1756-1791) had a passion for opera that manifested itself early in his childhood. At the age of twelve he composed his first opera, *Bastien und Bastienne*. In later years, when he served in the employ of the Archbishop von Colloredo, his patron's lack of interest in opera and the absence of an opera house in Salzburg became a source of frustration. After Mozart was dismissed from the Salzburg court, he settled in Vienna, a leading center for opera at that time. There, building on the contributions of Gluck and Antonio Salieri (1750-1825), Mozart pursued and perfected his vision of opera and demonstrated his unsurpassed genius.

For each of the three types of opera that Mozart wrote, give examples below:

Singspiel	*Opera seria*	*Opera buffa*
_____	_____	_____
_____	_____	_____
_____	_____	_____

Required Listening: Mozart, *The Marriage of Figaro* (Selections from Act One)

In writing *The Marriage of Figaro* (*Le Nozze di Figaro*), Mozart chose to set to music one of the most controversial plays of his time. Fully aware of the notoriety of the subject matter, he steered clear of the play's more subversive elements, focusing instead on the human conflict and intrigue. To this day, *The Marriage of Figaro* remains among the most popular and beloved operas of all time, admired for its impeccable craftsmanship, tender lyricism, farcical humor, and innovative use of ensembles.

Listen to the overture to *The Marriage of Figaro*, then listen to or watch a video performance of Scenes 6-7 from Act 1. If possible, follow a score while you listen. Answer the questions below and then complete the listening outlines for the Overture and Scenes 6-7 from Act 1:

Librettist _____ Type of opera _____

Author of the play upon which it is based _____

Why was this play so controversial at the time? _____

_____

_____

_____

Where was this opera first performed, and how was it received?

_____

_____

_____

Describe the principal characters and identify their voice types:

Character	Voice type	Brief description
Figaro	baritone	personal valet to the count
Susanna		
Cherubino		
Count Almaviva		
Countess Almaviva		
Basilio		
Doctor Bartolo		
Marcellina		
Barbarina		

Summarize the plot of this four-act opera.

_____

_____

_____

_____

_____

_____

_____

Overture

As was the custom of the day, *The Marriage of Figaro* begins with an overture. By Mozart's time, however, an orchestral form using the sonata-form principle had replaced the AB form of the French Overture that was customary in Baroque opera. Without actually quoting themes to come, this overture sets the mood for the drama that follows. (In the 19th century, opera overtures and preludes often used themes from the opera itself. The prelude to Bizet's *Carmen* illustrates this practice.)

Key _____   Meter _____   Tempo _____

Ex. 4.5. Mozart, Overture to *The Marriage of Figaro,* mm. 1-7.

This overture demonstrates Modified Sonata-Allegro form. What section normally present in a Sonata-Allegro form has been omitted here?

_____

Describe briefly the thematic material, musical character and key structure of the two principal sections. Where possible, comment on instrumentation.

Exposition _____

_____

_____

_____

_____

Recapitulation _____

_____

_____

_____

_____

How does this overture set the mood for the opera?

_____

_____

_____

Act 1, Scenes 6 and 7 (Aria, Recitative, and Trio)

Where in the palace does this scene take place? _____

Which characters appear in these scenes?

_____   _____

_____   _____

Aria: "Non so più"

Form _____ Key _____ Meter _____

Sung by _____

Ex. 4.6. Mozart, "Non so più," from *The Marriage of Figaro*, mm. 1-5.

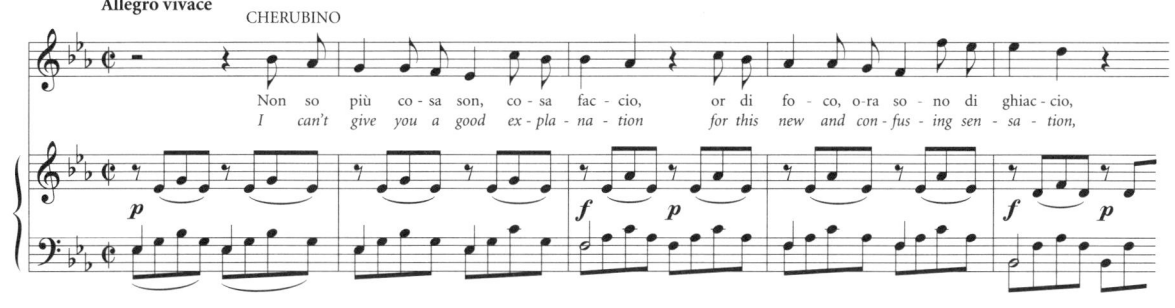

What sentiments are being expressed in this aria and how are they evoked musically?

_____

_____

_____

_____

_____

Recitative: "Ah! Son perduto!"

Type of recitative _____

Sung by   _____   _____

_____

Ex. 4.7. Mozart, "Ah! Son perduto," from *The Marriage of Figaro*, mm. 1-5.

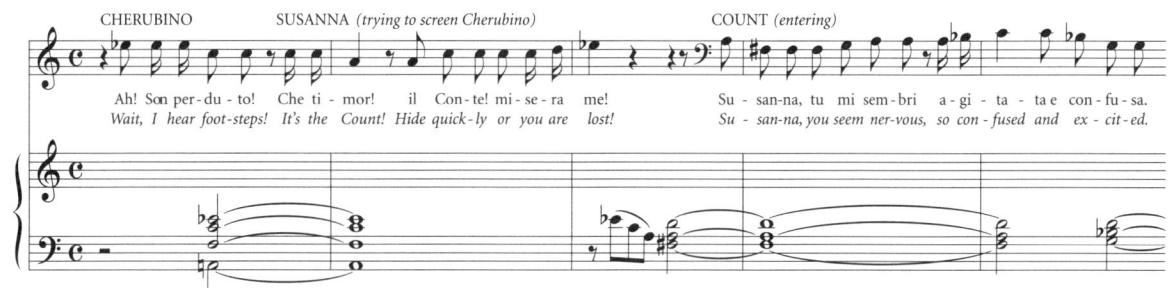

What comical situations take place as this scene unfolds?

___

Trio (Terzetto): "Cosa sento!"
Ex. 4.8. Mozart, "Cosa sento!" from *The Marriage of Figaro*, mm. 4-15.

What Classical form (typically used in instrumental music) is applied here?

___

What are the emotions expressed by each of the three characters in this exchange?

Count Almaviva ___

Basilio ___

Susanna ___

Based on your study of *The Marriage of Figaro,* list five characteristics of Mozart's musical style:

1. ___
2. ___
3. ___
4. ___
5. ___

 *The Marriage of Figaro* is the second play in a trilogy by Beaumarchais. The other two plays have also been set to music. Approximately thirty years after *The Marriage of Figaro,* Italian opera composer Gioacchino Rossini created *The Barber of Seville,* which he based on the first play of the trilogy. In 1991, American composer John Corigliano's opera *The Ghosts of Versailles* premiered at the Metropolitan Opera. This work was inspired by the final play in the trilogy and features the child of Susanna and Figaro and Beaumarchais himself as main characters.

Supplemental Activity: Viewing a Complete Performance of *The Marriage of Figaro*

To fully appreciate *The Marriage of Figaro*, watch a video performance of the entire opera. Listen especially for the following highlights:

Act One: "Non più andrai" (Figaro)
Act Two: "Porgi amor" (Countess)
            "Voi che sapete" (Cherubino)
Act Three: "Dove sono" (Countess)
            "Che soave zeffiretto" (Countess and Susanna)
Act Four: "Tutto è disposto…Aprite un po' queglo'occhi" (Figaro)
            Finale: *Scena Ultima*

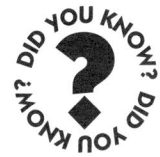 In the 1980s, the controversial international director Peter Sellars created three groundbreaking interpretations of the Mozart/da Ponte operas. He set *Così fan tutte* in a chrome and candy-colored 1950s diner, *Don Giovanni* in New York's Spanish Harlem, and *The Marriage of Figaro* in a fashionable Manhattan penthouse. In doing so, Sellars illustrated the timelessness of the stories, and gave audiences a fresh look at these enduring classics.

Recommended Listening for Opera:
G.F. Handel: "V'adoro pupille" from *Giulio Cesare*
             "Ombra mai fu" from *Xerxes*
             "Lascia ch'io pianga" from *Rinaldo*
C.W. Gluck: "Che farò senza Euridice" from *Orfeo ed Euridice*
W.A. Mozart: "Là ci darem la mano" and "Madamina, Il catalogo e questo"
             from *Don Giovanni*
             "Ach ich fühl's" and "Der Hölle Rache" from *The Magic Flute*

Cantata

Just as the patronage of the Roman Catholic Church fostered the evolution of the mass in the Middle Ages and Renaissance, the growth and development of the cantata is closely tied to the German Lutheran Church in the Baroque era.

When the Catholic priest Martin Luther defiantly posted his famous ninety-five theses on the door of the Palast Church in Wittenberg in 1517, he launched the Reformation movement in Germany. In documenting his complaints against the Church, Luther advocated many changes. Wanting to connect more closely with his parishioners, he proposed that the service in his new church be celebrated in German instead of Latin. Another way to engage the congregation was by replacing elaborate polyphonic settings of the traditional Latin mass with a new, more accessible kind of music: the German chorale.

With the adoption of chorales, the congregation could actively participate in the music of the service. Over time, the composers working within the Lutheran Church found ways to incorporate the chorale as a framing device in the cantata.

Building a Musical Vocabulary: *Cantata*

Define the following terms:

cantata

chorale

canon

fugue

augmentation

arioso

oboe da caccia

oboe d'amore _____

_____

_____

taille _____

_____

_____

Johann Sebastian Bach

Of the many Baroque composers who contributed to the development of the cantata, Johann Sebastian Bach (1685-1750) stands as a towering giant, both for his sheer output as well as his contrapuntal genius. Bach held several church positions in his lifetime, which gave him the opportunity to compose new cantatas for each week's Sunday service. As a result, he was able to refine and perfect his approach to the genre.

Approximately how many cantatas did Bach compose? _____

During which compositional period of his life did he compose the greatest number of cantatas? _____

Name two sacred cantatas by Bach other than No. 80. Give the number and title.

Cantata No. _____: "_____"

Cantata No. _____: "_____"

Name two secular cantatas by Bach.

1. _____   2. _____

Required Listening: Bach, *Cantata No. 80*, "Ein feste Burg ist unser Gott" (Selections)

This remarkable eight-movement choral work demonstrates a wide range of Bach's craftsmanship and artistry: contrapuntal ingenuity, mastery of large architectural structures, vocal lyricism, and word painting. It also stands as an enduring testament to his deep religious faith.

Listen to a recording of *Cantata No. 80*. If possible, follow a score as you listen. Fill in the blanks below, then complete the listening outlines for movements 1, 2, 5, and 8.

Translation of title _____

Original chorale (probably) by _____

Additional text written by _____

Language of text _____

Later revisions by _____

Approximate date of composition _____   Number of movements _____

Number of movements that use the chorale melody _____

Ex. 4.9. Bach, *Ein feste Burg ist unser Gott* (original chorale melody).

[Musical notation with text:]
Das Wort sie sol - len las - sen stahn und kein Dank da - zu___ ha - ben. Neh - men sie uns den
Er ist bei uns wohl auf__ dem Plan mit sei - nem Geist und__ Ga - ben.

Leib, Gut, Ehr', Kind und Weib, laß fah - ren da - hin, sie ha - bens kein__ Ge - winn, das Reich muß uns doch__ blei - ben.

How many phrases make up the original chorale? _____

How are phrases 1 and 3 related? _____

How are phrases 2, 4, and 9 related?

What is being expressed in the chorale text?

_____

_____

_____

The eight movements of this cantata are organized as follows, creating an arch-like structure:

⬛ 5 **Chorus:** Unison chorale

★ 4 **Aria:** Soprano solo

⬛ 6 **Recitative and Arioso:** Tenor solo

● 3 **Recitative and Arioso:** Bass solo

▲ 2 **Duet:** Soprano and bass soloists

▲ 7 **Duet:** Alto and tenor soloists

■ 1 **Chorus:** Choral fugue, based on chorale melody

■ 8 **Chorus:** 4-part chorale

Movement 1: Choral Fugue

Bach's contrapuntal ingenuity is demonstrated in this elaborate setting of Luther's original chorale tune. The well-known chorale melody would have been familiar to the congregation attending the Lutheran service at which it was first performed.

Key _____ Meter _____ Tempo _____

Original performing forces _____

_____

_____

What contributions did Wilhelm Friedemann Bach make to the orchestration after his father's death?

_____

What effect do you think is achieved by these additions?

_____

_____

The opening tenor melody is an embellished version of the original chorale. In Ex. 4.10, the circled notes show the original chorale tune.

Ex. 4.10. Bach, *Cantata No. 80*, First Movement, mm. 1-6.

In what manner does Bach present each phrase of the chorale in this movement?

_____

_____

In the brief interludes that connect each fugal exposition, canon and augmentation are featured. When Bach presents the second and fourth phrases with their respective fugal expositions, phrases 1 and 3 serve as counter-subjects. These are some examples of the contrapuntal ingenuity demonstrated in this opening movement.

Movement 2: Duet for Soprano and Bass

Key _____ Meter _____ Tempo _____

Performing forces _____

_____

Ex. 4.11. Bach, *Cantata No. 80*, Second Movement, mm. 10-13.

In Ex. 4.11, circle the notes of the original chorale tune, as was done in Ex. 4.10.

What is being expressed in the soprano text of the second movement?
_____
_____

What is being expressed in the bass text? _____
_____

As you observed in Ex. 4.11, the soprano is singing the decorated chorale melody. Describe the countermelody sung by the bass.
_____
_____
_____

Movement 5: Chorale for Unison Chorus

Key _____   Meter _____   Tempo _____

Performing forces _____
_____

Ex. 4.12. Bach, *Cantata No. 80*, Fifth Movement, mm. 13-17.

Und wenn die Welt voll Teu - fel wär,

What is being expressed in the text of the fifth movement?
_____
_____
_____

How is the chorale tune treated in this movement? What effect is created?
_____
_____
_____

Describe the instrumental accompaniment.
_____
_____
_____

Movement 8: Chorale

Key _____ Meter _____ Tempo _____

Performing forces _____

_____

How did Bach treat Luther's melody in this final movement?

_____

_____

On the recording you listened to, were the voices accompanied by instruments? If so, what material were they playing?

_____

_____

What is being expressed in the text? How does this text provide a fitting conclusion to this majestic work?

_____

_____

_____

Historians regard Bach's music as the pinnacle of achievement in a long tradition of contrapuntal writing. Based on your study of *Cantata No. 80*, list five style traits you have observed in his music:

1. *mastery of contrapuntal craft*
2. _____
3. _____
4. _____
5. _____

To what other musical genres did Bach make important contributions?

_____

_____

_____

_____

Recommended Listening for Cantata:
J.S. Bach: "Coffee" Cantata, BWV 211
              Cantata No. 140, "Wachet auf," BWV 140

Oratorio

The term *oratorio* is derived from the place in which these works were first performed: an oratory, or prayer room of a church. The origins of this sacred vocal genre can be traced to Italy in the late 16th century.

Building a Musical Vocabulary: *Oratorio*

Define *oratorio*. _____

_____

_____

Name three Baroque or Classical composers of oratorios, and list one composition title for each:

Composer	Title
1. _____	_____
2. _____	_____
3. _____	_____

The term *passion* is used to designate a particular type of oratorio. What is the subject matter of these works?

_____

_____

Name two passions by J.S. Bach.

_____   _____

Franz Joseph Haydn

After Franz Joseph Haydn (1732-1809) retired from his long-held post at the Esterházy palace, he made two historic visits to London, first in 1791-1792, and again in 1794-1795. On these occasions, he developed an admiration for Handel's English oratorios and rekindled his love of choral music. Upon his return to Austria, Haydn was inspired to compose his own majestic contributions to the oratorio genre: *The Creation* and *The Seasons*.

Required Listening: Haydn, *The Creation* (Selections)

Listen to or watch a performance of *The Creation*. If possible, follow a score. Answer the questions below and then complete the listening outline for Part One, Scene Three:

Year of its premiere _____

Genre _____

Librettist (German) _____

Sources of text 1) _____

2) _____

What do Milton's verses add to the presentation of the creation story?

_____
_____
_____
_____

Performing forces _____
_____

Outline the overall structure of *The Creation*.

_____

The Overture is entitled "The Representation of Chaos." How does Haydn evoke the image suggested by the title?

_____
_____
_____

List the voice types for the main characters:

Characters		Voice type
Adam		_____
Eve		_____
Three Archangels:	Raphael	_____
	Uriel	_____
	Gabriel	_____

Part One, Scene Three

Which parts of the Genesis story are presented in this section?

_____
_____

Uriel's Recitative (No. 12): "And God said: Let there be light"

What type of recitative is this? _____

How is the word "light" depicted in this musical setting?
_____
_____

Uriel's Recitative (No. 13): "In splendor bright"

Ex. 4.13. Haydn, "In splendor bright," from *The Creation*, mm. 1-15.

Ex. 4.13 shows the brief orchestral interlude that precedes this recitative. Within this section, how does Haydn evoke the splendor of the rising sun?
_____
_____
_____

What type of recitative is this? _____

What makes Haydn's settings of the following passages in this recitative so effective?

"In splendor bright" _____
_____

"With softer beams" _____
_____

"The space immense of the azure sky" _____
_____

Chorus and Trio (No. 14): "The heavens are telling the Glory of God"

Key _____   Meter _____

This section is organized as follows: Chorus – Trio – Chorus – Trio – Chorus

Ex. 4.14. Haydn, "The heavens are telling the Glory of God" from *The Creation*, mm. 1-4.

How does Haydn achieve a sense of grandeur in the opening chorus?
_____
_____
_____

In the short Trio that follows the chorus, identify one effective use of word painting.
_____
_____
_____

After the Trio, how is the return of the chorus handled differently from the opening chorus shown in Ex. 4.14?
_____
_____
_____

After the return of the chorus, another Trio, "In all the lands..." follows. Describe an additional effective use of word painting exhibited in this passage.

_____

_____

_____

_____

How is the final statement of the chorus varied and what impression does it make on the listener?

_____

_____

Recommended Listening for Oratorio:
G.F. Handel: "He spake the word and there came all manner of flies" from *Israel In Egypt*
"For unto us a Child is born" from *Messiah*
F.J. Haydn: "From Aries now... With joy th'impatient husbandsman" and "O welcome now ye shady groves...What refreshment to the senses" from *The Seasons*

Supplemental Activity: "The Movies Go to the Opera"

Of the three Baroque and Classical vocal forms you have studied, opera is without question the one that enjoyed the most popularity in the eras that followed. Composers of the 19th and 20th centuries continued to cultivate and refine the genre, and enthusiastic audiences continue to attend live performances today. In recent years, music from operas has been featured in numerous "box-office hits." The CD *The Movies Go to the Opera* (EMI 7777-69596-2) features operatic excerpts used in movies such as *Moonstruck, Fatal Attraction, The Witches of Eastwick, A Room with a View, Apocalypse Now,* and *Hannah and Her Sisters*.

You may find it interesting to sample the effect created by the use of operatic excerpts when they appear in the context of popular movies or television shows. Watch one of the films listed above, or have your teacher recommend another movie that incorporates music from an opera.

Movie title _____

Opera excerpt(s) used _____

_____

_____

Comments _____
_____
_____
_____

Review and Reflection

Opera, oratorio, and cantata are three genres of vocal music that share many similar characteristics and features. At the same time, each has its own distinct character.

Compare and contrast the three genres by filling in the chart below:

	Opera	**Oratorio**	**Cantata**
Performing forces	Soloists, chorus, orchestra		
Presentation	Staged with scenery, costumes, acting	Not staged	Not staged
Musical components	Overture, Recitative, aria, ensemble, chorus		
Origins			
Composers			
Examples (composition titles)			

Of the works you studied in this unit, which did you enjoy the most and why?

_____
_____
_____
_____

Exploring Music History: A Guided Approach

Quiz

1. For each of the musical elements listed below, name a work that contains or demonstrates it. Draw your examples from the works you have studied in this unit.

	Title of complete work	**Title of specific musical number**
ground bass	Dido and Aeneas	Aria: "When I am laid in earth"
"trouser role"	_____	_____
recitativo secco	_____	_____
SATB chorus	_____	_____
word painting	_____	_____
castrato part	_____	_____

2. For each of the librettists listed below, name a musical composition and its corresponding composer.

	Title of work	**Composer**
Nahum Tate	_____	_____
Giovanni Busenello	_____	_____
Lorenzo da Ponte	_____	_____
Salomo Franck	_____	_____
Gottfried von Swieten	_____	_____

UNIT FIVE

INSTRUMENTAL MUSIC OF THE MIDDLE AGES, RENAISSANCE, AND BAROQUE

Timeline

	MIDDLE AGES	RENAISSANCE	BAROQUE
	A.D. 476	1450	1600 — 1750
GENRES		Dance music	
		Keyboard music	
			Suite ....
			Concerto ....
COMPOSERS	"Anonymous"		
		Tielman Susato	
			Domenico Scarlatti
			George Frideric Handel
			Johann Sebastian Bach

The Role of Instrumental Music in the Middle Ages and Renaissance

As you have already discovered, there is a substantial legacy of notated vocal music from the Middle Ages and Renaissance in the form of both sacred and secular manuscripts. In the realm of instrumental music, however, this is not the case. While we are aware that a rich and vibrant tradition existed (as evidenced by written accounts, artist depictions, and existing instruments), instrumental music was typically not documented.

Why do you think this discrepancy exists? _____

_____

_____

Consider how each of the factors below inhibited the development of notation with respect to instrumental music:

Attitude of the Roman Catholic Church towards instruments _____

_____

_____

Exploring Music History: A Guided Approach   Volume 2: Middle Ages to Classical

Role of instruments in accompanying singers _____

_____

_____

Nature of instrument construction _____

_____

_____

Availability of instruments _____

_____

_____

In the Middle Ages and Renaissance, instrumental music fulfilled specific roles and functions in society. List five ways in which instruments were used:

1. _accompanying singers_
2. _____
3. _____
4. _____
5. _____

Indoor and Outdoor Instruments

Although we currently categorize instruments into families based on their design and materials (strings, woodwinds, brass), this was not the case in the Middle Ages and Renaissance. Instruments were designated according to practical considerations that included volume capacity, tone quality, and appropriate venue for use. They were classified as either "indoor" or "outdoor."

What French words were used for these two categories?

Indoor _____

Outdoor _____

For each instrument below, identify the historical designation (indoor or outdoor) and, where possible, name the modern instrument into which each evolved:

Original instrument	Designation	Modern equivalent
Cornetto		
Crumhorn		
Dulcimer		
Handbells		

Volume 2: Middle Ages to Classical   Exploring Music History: A Guided Approach

Harp	_____	_____
Hurdy-gurdy	_____	_____
Lute	_____	_____
Nakers	_____	_____
Psaltery	_____	_____
Rebec	_____	_____
Recorder	_____	_____
Sackbut	_____	_____
Shawm	_____	_____
Slide trumpet	_____	_____
Tabor	_____	_____
Tambourine	_____	_____
Vielle	_____	_____
Viola da gamba	_____	_____

Despite their opposing classifications, it was not uncommon to combine indoor and outdoor instruments together in a single performance. You will discover this in your listening experience.

Use the internet to learn more about the early history of instrumental music. Conduct a search on the key words "Medieval instruments" and sample some of the many websites that show pictures. Be sure to explore any sites that provide audio clips so you can hear the unique sound qualities of these instruments.

Name three sources of information on which our knowledge of medieval and Renaissance instrumental music is based:

1. <u>original instruments which have survived and are preserved in museum collections</u>

2. _____

3. _____

Suggest three reasons why it would have been impractical for early composers to specify instrumentation in their scores:

1. <u>not all instruments were readily available</u>

2. _____

3. _____

Dance Music

In most world cultures, dancing has been a popular form of entertainment enjoyed by all social classes. One of the earliest documented collections of dance pieces is the *Chansonnier du Roy*, a French manuscript from the late 13th century. This collection contained troubadour and trouvère songs, as well as eight dances.

What is the English translation of *Chansonnier du Roy*? _____

_____

Building a Musical Vocabulary: *Dance Music*

For each dance listed below, explain the origins and outline the musical characteristics:

estampie _____

_____

_____

galliard _____

_____

_____

pavane _____

_____

_____

basse danse _____

_____

_____

branle _____

_____

_____

saltarello _____

_____

_____

ronde _____

_____

_____

Define each of the following terms as they relate to early instrumental music:

consort of instruments _____

_____

musica ficta _____

_____

drone _____

_____

embellishment _____

_____

Required Listening: Anonymous, *Royal Estampie No. 4* from *Chansonnier du Roy*

The *estampie*, a stately dance involving elaborate body movements, is one of the earliest dance types. (The oldest surviving *estampie* is *Kalenda maya*, a dance-song by troubadour Raimbault de Vaqueiras.)

Listen to a recording of *Royal Estampie No. 4*. If possible, follow a score as you listen. Answer the questions below:

Ex. 5.1. Anonymous, *Royal Estampie No. 4* (first section) from *Chansonnier du Roy*.

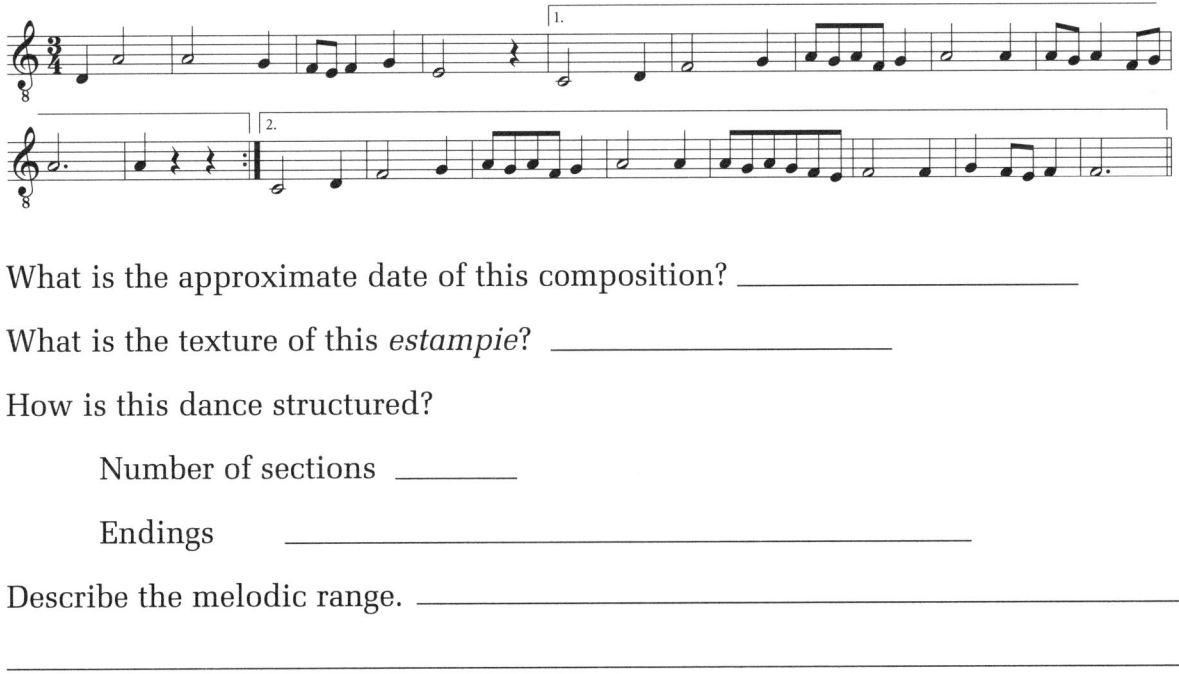

What is the approximate date of this composition? _____

What is the texture of this *estampie*? _____

How is this dance structured?

    Number of sections _____

    Endings _____

Describe the melodic range. _____

_____

Although this *estampie* consists of only a single line melody in its notated form, in the recording you listened to there may have been some improvised accompaniment. This is in keeping with what historians believe was the performance practice of the time. How was the monophonic melody supported in your recording?

_____
_____

If you followed a score, did your recording render the notated melody exactly? Describe any use of embellishment.

_____
_____

Name the instruments used in the recording you listened to, and classify them according to their historical designation:

Instrument name	Classification (Indoor/Outdoor)
_____	_____
_____	_____
_____	_____
_____	_____
_____	_____

For each section in *Royal Estampie No. 4*, identify the featured instrument and texture.

_____
_____
_____
_____
_____
_____

Music Publishing in the Renaissance

The invention of the printing press in the 15th century by Johann Gutenberg, like the personal computer in the latter part of the 20th century, had an extraordinary impact on all aspects of western culture, including music. It was only natural that the previously arduous and costly task of copying music by hand would be replaced by mechanical reproduction, which was quicker and more cost-efficient. As a result of this invention, music became more widely available and there was a greater understanding and exchange of international styles and influences.

Name three leading centers for music printing in the Renaissance.

1. Antwerp

2. _____

3. _____

 The invention of the printing press was among the most significant events of the early Renaissance. Not surprisingly, the first document born of this new technology was the Bible. Using a search engine and the key words "Gutenberg Bible," search the internet for more information and pictures of these rare examples of early printing. Where might you go to see an original Gutenberg Bible on display?

Tielman Susato and *Danserye*

Tielman Susato (*ca* 1515-1567) was a composer, instrumentalist, and publisher based in Antwerp, Belgium. He was particularly active in publishing the works of Franco-Flemish masters such as Roland de Lassus (1532-1594). His collection *Danserye* contains examples of many of the popular dances of the time.

Name five dances contained in *Danserye*.

_____ _____ _____

_____ _____

The title page of the *Danserye* contains the following inscription: "Fit to be played on all instruments." This indication is a clear sign that composers did not yet specify exact instrumentation. Why was this the case?

_____

_____

_____

Required Listening: Pavane "Mille regretz" AND Ronde I and Ronde II (from *Danserye*)

In Renaissance vocal music, the four principal vocal ranges we are familiar with today (soprano, alto, tenor, and bass) emerged. Likewise, ranges and designations were created in instrumental consorts—soprano, alto, tenor, and bass recorders, for example. These principles are clearly reflected in the dances from the *Danserye*.

Listen to Pavane "Mille regretz" AND Ronde I and Ronde II from *Danserye*. If possible, follow a score. Complete the listening outlines below:

Pavane "Mille regretz"

Ex. 5.2. Pavane "Mille regretz," from *Danserye*, mm. 1-8.

What is the meter of this dance? _____

What is the formal structure? _____

Give the English translation for the words "mille regretz." _____

Who wrote the original chanson (of the same name) on which this dance was based? _____

This work demonstrates *musica ficta*. In Ex. 5.2, locate the sign that indicates this practice.

Answer the following questions about the recording you heard:

What instruments did the performers use?

_____
_____
_____

Did the performers supply additional ornaments? If so, how were they applied?

_____
_____
_____

Describe the tempo chosen by the performers. _____
_____

Ronde I

Ex. 5.3. Ronde I from *Danserye*, mm. 1-4.

What is the meter of this dance? _____

What is the formal structure? _____

Answer the following questions about the recording you heard:

What instruments did the performers use?

_____

_____

_____

_____

Did the performers supply additional ornaments? If so, how were they applied?

_____

_____

_____

Describe the tempo chosen by the performers. _____

_____

Ronde II

Ex. 5.4. Ronde II from *Danserye*, mm. 1-4.

Exploring Music History: A Guided Approach Volume 2: Middle Ages to Classical

What is the meter of this dance? _____

What is the formal structure? _____

Answer the following questions about the recording you heard:

What instruments did the performers use?

_____

_____

_____

Did the performers supply additional ornaments? If so, how were they applied?

_____

_____

_____

Describe the tempo chosen by the performers. _____

_____

At the conclusion of Ronde II, did the performers repeat Ronde I? If so, what larger form did this create? _____

> **Did you know?** In the Middle Ages and Renaissance, the tritone (augmented 4th or diminished 5th) was referred to as *diabolus in musica* or "the devil in music." This interval was typically avoided because of its angular dissonance. The application of *musica ficta* helped to soften the unwanted dissonances, often by transforming objectionable augmented 4ths into consonant perfect 4ths.

Supplemental Activity: *Listening to the Chanson "Mille regretz"*

Listen to a recording of the original chanson "Mille regretz" by Josquin des Prez.

In what language was the text sung? _____

Translate the title into English. _____

How many voices are used? _____

If possible, summarize the meaning of the poem:

_____

_____

Describe the musical character of the chanson.

_____

_____

_____

How much of the original character was retained in the instrumental version?

_____

_____

_____

Recommended Listening for Dance Music:
Anonymous: *Galliarde*
Ronde & Quatre branles

Note: The above examples are included in the recording *At the Sign of the Crumhorn: Flemish Songs and Dance Music from the Susato Music Books* (see Appendix B).

Keyboard Music

Keyboard instruments are extremely popular today, but their appeal is not a new phenomenon. The origins of the keyboard can be traced back to the earliest days of the Roman Catholic Church, when the organ enjoyed an exalted position. As additional keyboard instruments were developed during the Renaissance and Baroque periods, the German word *clavier* was used. This term specified keyboard instruments other than the organ.

Building a Musical Vocabulary: *Early Keyboard Instruments*

Briefly describe the three types of organs identified below:

portative _____

_____

positive _____

_____

regal _____

_____

Briefly describe the following instruments, paying close attention to how the sound was generated by each:

clavichord _____
_____

harpsichord _____
_____

cembalo _____
_____

clavecin _____
_____

virginal _____
_____

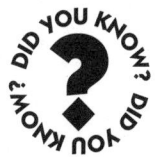 The earliest notated music for keyboard dates back to 1325 and is found in the *Robertsbridge Codex*. Unlike later keyboard music, the pieces in this collection are not idiomatic. Included are arrangements based on vocal models, and dances in the Italian style. The pieces were written for instruments that had a range of just over two octaves.

The *Fitzwilliam Virginal Book*

The *Fitzwilliam Virginal Book* is a historically significant keyboard collection dating from the early 17th century. It was named after Viscount Fitzwilliam, the generous patron who donated the manuscript to Cambridge University in 1816. Represented in the collection are the principal English composers of the late Renaissance, including William Byrd, John Bull, Thomas Morley, and Giles Farnaby.

The charming keyboard works contained in the *Fitzwilliam Virginal Book* include dances, arrangements of songs and madrigals, and variations. This collection contains almost 300 pieces and provides us with evidence of an increasingly idiomatic writing style for the keyboard. One can see that the virtuosic potential of the instrument was being explored and exploited through the use of rapid scale passages, ornamentation, and many novel figurations.

 Keyboard instruments in the Renaissance were often far more decorative in appearance than their modern counterparts. Using your search engine and the keywords "Fitzwilliam Virginal Book" and "Renaissance keyboard instruments," explore the beauty of these historical instruments. Listen to sound clips if possible, and learn more about their construction, design, shape, and size.

Building a Musical Vocabulary: *Early Keyboard Genres*

Summarize the principal characteristics of each of the following keyboard forms:

prelude _____
_____
_____

passacaglia _____
_____
_____

toccata _____
_____
_____

fantasia _____
_____
_____

chorale prelude _____
_____
_____

chorale variations _____
_____
_____

sonata _____
_____
_____

binary form _____
_____
_____

Domenico Scarlatti

It is an interesting coincidence that three great masters of the Baroque era, J.S. Bach, G.F. Handel, and Domenico Scarlatti (1685-1757) were born in the same year. Like his father, Alessandro, Domenico Scarlatti composed Italian operas. Today, however, his fame rests almost entirely on his brilliant keyboard sonatas.

Scarlatti wrote over five hundred single-movement sonatas that were originally titled *Esercizi per gravicembalo*. Much like etudes, they each present at least one recurring technical challenge. Many are quite virtuosic and feature hand crossings, arpeggiated figures, ornaments, repeated notes, and rapid passagework. Most of these sonatas exhibit binary form, yet at the same time they foreshadow the Sonata-Allegro structure that became so important in the Classical period.

What is the English translation of *Esercizi per gravicembalo*?
_____

What do the letters L and K stand for in Scarlatti sonata titles, and what do they signify?

L _____

K _____

Required Listening: Scarlatti, *Sonata in D Minor*, L 413, K 9 OR *Sonata in D Major*, L 463, K 430

Listen to **EITHER** *Sonata in D Minor*, L 413, K 9 **OR** *Sonata in D Major*, L 463, K 430. If possible, follow a score as you listen. (These works are in *Celebration Series®, The Piano Odyssey®, Repertoire Album 9.*)

Answer the following questions for the sonata you have chosen:

Title _____

Meter _____

Tempo indication _____

What is the formal design of the sonata you studied? In the space provided, draw a diagram to illustrate the structure, including principal keys and modulations.

[   ]

From the list below, circle the idiomatic features that are evident in the sonata you studied:

acciaccaturas	rapid passagework
arpeggio figuration	sequential writing
dissonant harmony	suspensions
hand crossing	syncopation
pedal point	trills and mordents

How do these devices serve to project the musical character of this sonata?

___

Based on your study of this work and your previous studies of works by J.S. Bach, what aspects of Scarlatti's musical style are different from that of his famous contemporary?

___

Recommended Listening for Early Keyboard Music:
Fitzwilliam Virginal Book:
    Thomas Morley: *Goe from my Window*
    William Byrd: *The Carman's Whistle*
    John Bull: *The King's Hunt*
    Giles Farnaby: *Giles Farnaby's Dream*
J.S. Bach: Chorale Prelude, *Ein feste Burg ist unser Gott*, Anh. II 49
    Organ Toccata and Fugue in D Minor, BWV 565
G.F. Handel: *Passacaglia in G Minor* from *Keyboard Suite No. 1*
    "The Harmonious Blacksmith" from *Clavier Suite No. 5*

Baroque Keyboard Works in *Celebration Series*®, *The Piano Odyssey*®:
J.S. Bach: *Little Prelude in E Minor*, BWV 938 (*Piano Repertoire 8*)
J.S. Bach: *Little Prelude in D Major*, BWV 936 (*Piano Repertoire 8*)
G.P. Telemann: *Fantasia in D Minor*, TWV 33:2 (*Piano Repertoire 8*)
D. Scarlatti: *Sonata in C Major*, L 104, K 159 (*Piano Repertoire 9*)
    Sonata in D Minor, L 413, K 9 (*Piano Repertoire 9*)
    Sonata in D Major, L 463, K 430 (*Piano Repertoire 9*)

Supplemental Activity: *Exploring the Artistry of Glenn Gould*

Internationally acclaimed Canadian pianist Glenn Gould (1932-1982) remains a towering figure among 20th-century musicians. Though he is best known for his unique and deeply personal interpretations of the music of J.S. Bach, Gould left a rich and varied legacy of recordings and writings. Despite great successes as a concert pianist, Gould gave his last public performance in 1964. From that point on, he deliberately chose to explore the possibilities of recording technology in favor of live performance. In this respect his role was that of a pioneer.

To become more familiar with the outstanding accomplishments of Glenn Gould, choose one or more of the activities suggested below:

1) Using your internet search engine and the keywords "Glenn Gould," explore the life and musical career of this intriguing figure.

2) Watch the renowned Canadian film *32 Short Films About Glenn Gould*, directed by François Girard and starring Colm Feore.

3) Gould recorded Bach's *Goldberg Variations* twice, once at the very beginning of his career, and again in 1981, only a year before he died. Listen to one or both of these very different recordings.

Suite

Originally, dance music served a very practical function, but over time it gradually evolved into a stylized art form. Dance music was no longer intended just for dancing, but it was also enjoyed for the listening pleasure it provided.

In the Renaissance era dances were often paired to emphasize contrast, as in the Pavane and Galliard combination. In the Baroque era, the grouping of contrasting dance pieces was taken a step further with the establishment of the formal dance suite. The titles of dances that were popular during the Renaissance hint at a growing internationalism emerging in the style. This international focus continued, and is clearly evident in the four standard dances of the Baroque suite.

Building a Musical Vocabulary: *Baroque Dance Suite*

Explain the national origins of each of the following dances, and outline the musical characteristics of each (form, meter, character, etc.):

Standard dances

allemande _____

_____

_____

courante _____

_____

_____

sarabande _____

_____

_____

gigue _____

_____

_____

Optional dances and movements

menuet _____
_____
_____

bourrée _____
_____
_____

gavotte _____
_____
_____

hornpipe _____
_____
_____

air _____
_____
_____

Explain the following terms as they relate to the Baroque suite:

ordre _____
_____
_____

double _____
_____
_____

ornamentation _____
_____
_____

Throughout the ages, dancing has always been a popular form of entertainment, social interaction, and just plain fun! Although the enjoyment of this activity has not diminished, the approach and style now is very different than it was in the Baroque period. Search the internet for pictures and video clips that illustrate some of the dances you have encountered in your studies. Use the key words "Baroque dances."

Exploring Music History: A Guided Approach   Volume 2: Middle Ages to Classical

George Frideric Handel

George Frideric Handel (1685-1759) was a versatile, cosmopolitan musician with talents in many areas. His conducting skills and his keyboard virtuosity (particularly on the organ) enabled him to produce first-rate works in a wide array of genres. Handel's career also embodied the internationalism that characterized the early 18th century. For example, he devoted much of his energy to bringing Italian opera to English aristocratic audiences. Alongside his dramatic works, there also exists a large body of instrumental music that grew out of his association with his royal patrons Queen Anne, King George I, and King George II.

Required Listening: Handel, *Water Music* (Selections)

Despite the fact that it was originally composed for outdoor performances, to this day Handel's *Water Music* continues to be a staple at festive occasions such as weddings and formal gatherings.

When was this work composed? _____

How many suites comprise *Water Music*? _____

How many movements are there in total? _____

What special circumstances surrounding the first performance of this work led to the designation "Water Music"?

_____

Which instrument did not make the voyage? _____

What type of overture opens *Water Music*? _____

Listen to a recording of the "Allegro" and "Hornpipe" from the *Water Music Suite in D Major*. If possible, follow a score as you listen. Complete the listening outlines below:

Allegro

In addition to the traditional dance movements, many Baroque composers included non-dance movements in their suites to add variety. This spirited Allegro is one such movement.

Key _____ Meter _____ Form _____

Ex. 5.5. Handel, "Allegro" from *Water Music Suite in D Major*, mm. 1-5.

Section A

Which instruments play the opening theme? _____

Describe the character of the opening theme and the harmonies outlined.

_____
_____
_____

How is a regal atmosphere conveyed in this section?
a) prominent use of brass instruments
b) pompous dotted rhythms
c) use of ground bass

Which instruments are in dialogue?
a) trumpets and violins
b) oboes and cellos
c) flutes and harpsichord

What material is alternated in dialogue?
- a) ascending scales and descending scales
- b) ascending scales and descending chord figures
- c) descending scales and ascending chord figures

Section B

How is rhythmic contrast achieved in this section? _____

_____

How is this section orchestrated? _____

_____

When Section A returns, how is it varied and altered? _____

_____

How is this movement linked to the next? _____

Hornpipe

Key _____ Meter _____ Tempo _____

Form _____

Ex. 5.6. Handel, "Hornpipe" from *Water Music Suite in D Major*, mm. 1-11.

Section A

What rhythmic device contributes to the majestic musical character in this festive opening?

_____

Which families of instruments are in dialogue in this section?

_____

_____

Section B

Name the key of Section B and its relationship to the home key.

_____

How does the character here contrast with Section A? _____

_____

Which group of instruments is not present in Section B? _____

What rhythmic device from Section A is employed in Section B in the

woodwind parts? _____

What is the thematic connection between the material presented in Sections A and B?

_____

_____

How does the movement conclude? _____

_____

Describe the use of ornamentation in both movements. _____

_____

Why do you think this work received the enthusiastic reception that it did?

_____

_____

Recommended Listening for Baroque Suite:
G.F. Handel: *Music for the Royal Fireworks*
J.S. Bach: *Orchestral Suite No. 4 in D Major*, BWV 1069
    English Suite in G Minor, BWV 808
    Partita in B flat Major, BWV 825

Suite Movements in *Celebration Series®, The Piano Odyssey®*:
J.S. Bach: "Allemande and Gigue" from *French Suite No. 5*, BWV 816
  (*Piano Repertoire 10*)
G.F. Handel: "Allemande and Gigue" from *Suite No. 8 in F Minor*, HWV 433
  (*Piano Repertoire 10*)

 During the Baroque era, makers of string instruments (known as *luthiers*) achieved the highest level of excellence as illustrated by the fine craftsmanship of violinmakers Stradivarius, Guarneri, and Amati. Using your search engine, enter the names of these famous instrument makers to learn more about them and to find out which artists are using their instruments today.

Concerto

While composers in the Middle Ages and Renaissance often modeled their instrumental compositions after existing vocal works, Baroque composers developed many new instrumental forms independent of vocal models. Instrumental music became more important in the Baroque era, and for the first time, music written specifically for instruments attained the same level of significance as vocal music. At the same time, the approach to composing for instruments had evolved to include even more idiomatic writing and greater heights of virtuosity.

Chief among the new instrumental genres in the Baroque period was the *concerto*. Thousands of concertos were composed by such leading figures as Albinoni, J.S. Bach, Corelli, Handel, Torelli, and Vivaldi. In their works, they explored new formal constructions, innovative timbres (colors) and at times highly virtuosic playing. The large body of music produced by these Baroque masters laid the foundation for Classical and Romantic concertos.

The word *concerto* is Italian in origin. What is the literal translation of this word?

___

(The plural of *concerto* is *concerti*. However, in English, it is also appropriate to say "concertos.")

Building a Musical Vocabulary: *Baroque Concerto*

Define the following terms as they relate to the Baroque concerto:

solo concerto ___

___

___

concerto grosso _____

_____

_____

concertino _____

_____

_____

ripieno _____

_____

_____

ritornello form _____

_____

_____

figured bass _____

_____

_____

Johann Sebastian Bach

Johann Sebastian Bach (1685-1750) was employed at Cöthen from 1717-1723. During his tenure there, his employer Prince Leopold did not require a large body of music for the church. However, Leopold's fondness for instrumental music motivated Bach to compose a wealth of suites, keyboard works, and concertos.

Required Listening: Bach, *Brandenburg Concerto No. 2 in F Major*, BWV 1047

In 1719, Bach made the acquaintance of a visiting dignitary, the Margrave of Brandenburg, and in 1721, he humbly dedicated a set of six concertos to him. These works, known as the "Brandenburg Concertos," are among Bach's most beloved and recognized instrumental compositions.

Listen to a recording of *Brandenburg Concerto No. 2 in F Major*. If possible, follow a score as you listen. Answer the questions below and then complete the listening outlines for each movement:

When was this concerto written? _____

Which instruments form the *concertino*? _____ _____ _____ _____

What other instruments make up the orchestra? _____

First Movement

Key _____ Meter _____

Ex. 5.7. Bach, *Brandenburg Concerto No. 2 in F Major*, First Movement, mm. 1-8.

What is the formal design of this movement? _____

The members of the *concertino* play throughout the movement, sometimes as members of the *ripieno* and other times as soloists. How does Bach clarify for the listener which role these instruments play at any given moment?

_____

_____

What is the prevalent mood of this movement? _____

In Baroque music, there is often one underlying mood or "affect" dominating a movement or section. How is this principle evident in this work?

_____

_____

How does Bach achieve contrast within the movement?

_____

_____

_____

To which closely related keys does this movement modulate?

_____

Prior to the final *ritornello,* the rhythmic drive is momentarily arrested. In what key does the orchestra come to a cadence? _____

The type of melodic writing used in this movement is often described by the German word *Fortspinnung,* meaning "spinning forward." Now that you have listened to this movement, comment on the role that this melodic element plays in this composition.

_____

_____

_____

Second Movement

Key _____ Relationship to home key _____

Meter _____ Tempo _____

Besides using a contrasting key, meter, and tempo, how else did Bach create a new character in this movement?

_____

_____

_____

_____

Third Movement

Key _____ Meter _____ Tempo _____

Bach is famous for the formal structure that serves as the basis of this movement. What is the structure? _____

How many voices are presented? _____

In which order do the *concertino* instruments appear?

_____

Which soloist (omitted from the second movement) opens and closes this cheerful movement? _____

 Even though he is forever associated with the title of the *Brandenburg Concertos*, apparently the Margrave of Brandenburg never bothered to display Bach's musical gift or have the music performed. The manuscript—still in its wrapped scroll—was discovered among Brandenburg's personal effects after his death. The entire set of concertos was sold for a meager sum in 1734.

Recommended Listening for Baroque Concerto:
J.S. Bach: *Brandenburg Concertos*, Nos. 1, 3, 4, 5, 6, BWV 1046-1051
    Italian Concerto, BWV 971
    Concerto for Two Violins and Orchestra in D Minor, BWV 1044
    Concerto for Four Harpsichords and Orchestra, BWV 1065
Arcangelo Corelli: *Concerto*, op. 6, no. 8, "Christmas"
G.F. Handel: *Six Concerto Grossos*, op. 3

Supplemental Activity: *Comparing Baroque and Modern Performance Practice*

Currently there is an avid and enthusiastic interest in reconstructing authentic performances of early music. One world-renowned ensemble that specializes in Baroque performance is the Toronto-based Tafelmusik.

Name two other modern performers or ensembles that specialize in the performance of Baroque music:

_____   _____

Compare two recordings of one of the Baroque instrumental works from this unit. Listen to one version performed on period instruments, and one performed on modern instruments.

Recording No. 1:

Ensemble _____

Conductor _____

Comments _____

_____

_____

Recording No. 2:

Ensemble _____

Conductor _____

Comments _____

_____

_____

What differences did you observe? _____

_____

_____

_____

_____

Which version did you prefer, and why? _____

_____

_____

_____

_____

Review and Reflection

For each of the three eras you explored in this unit, summarize the role of instruments and instrumental music, genres cultivated, forms developed, and major composers. Include personal reflections and opinions about the music of each era.

Middle Ages

_____
_____
_____
_____
_____
_____
_____
_____

Renaissance

_____
_____
_____
_____
_____
_____
_____
_____

Baroque

_____
_____
_____
_____
_____
_____
_____
_____

Of the works you studied in this unit, which did you enjoy the most and why?

_____
_____
_____
_____

Quiz

1. For each musical element listed below, name a work that contains or demonstrates it. Choose your answers from the works you have studied in this unit.

	Title	**Composer**
ritornello	Brandenburg Concerto No. 2	J. S. Bach
musica ficta	_____	_____
monophonic melody	_____	_____
acciaccatura	_____	_____
binary form	_____	_____
ripieno	_____	_____

2. Give examples for each of the following:

   Two Renaissance dances _____
   _____

   Four standard dances in the Baroque suite _____
   _____
   _____
   _____

   Two composers represented in the *Fitzwilliam Virginal Book* _____
   _____

   Two Baroque keyboard forms _____
   _____

UNIT SIX

INSTRUMENTAL MUSIC OF THE CLASSICAL ERA

Timeline

1750	1770		1825
	CLASSICAL		
Pre-Classical			
Rococo – Style Galant			
GENRES			
Symphony ·			
Sonata ·			
Concerto ·			
Chamber Music ·			
COMPOSERS			
Mannheim School			
Sons of Johann Sebastian Bach			
Franz Joseph Haydn			
Wolfgang Amadeus Mozart			
Ludwig van Beethoven			
		Franz Schubert	

Symphony

In the early 18th century, the string orchestra supported by continuo became a standard performing ensemble. Some composers, including Handel and J.S. Bach, also explored the use of wind instruments. These experiments set the stage for the emergence of the modern symphony orchestra with its four instrumental families: strings, woodwinds, brass, and percussion.

In the Classical era, the symphony emerged as the dominant form in instrumental music. Between them, the three Viennese masters (Haydn, Mozart, and Beethoven) created over 150 symphonies, thereby laying the cornerstone of the orchestral repertoire.

C.P.E. Bach and the Pre-Classical Style

At the same time as J.S. Bach was completing his life's work, his four sons were already forging a musical style quite different from their father's.

Give the full names of the four musical sons of J.S. Bach, matching names to the dates provided:

(1710-1784) _____

(1714-1788) _____

(1732-1795) _____

(1735-1782) _____

Exploring Music History: A Guided Approach   Volume 2: Middle Ages to Classical

Carl Philip Emmanuel Bach's works include twenty symphonies, numerous keyboard sonatas and concertos, and over three hundred songs. Summarize his musical contributions under the following headings:

formal design _____
_____
_____

musical genres cultivated _____
_____
_____

idiomatic keyboard style _____
_____
_____

C.P.E. Bach is also remembered for his treatise, *Essay on the True Art of Playing Keyboard Instruments* (1753). Describe the contents of this important work.

_____
_____
_____

Translate and explain *Empfindsamkeit:*

   Translation _____

   Explanation _____

Translate and explain *Sturm und Drang:*

   Translation _____

   Explanation _____

Translate and explain *Style Galant:*

   Translation _____

   Explanation _____

Explain the origins and meaning of the term *Rococo:*

_____
_____

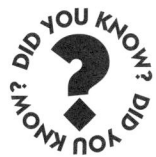 In the 1750s, C.P.E. Bach was in the employ of Frederick the Great, as was the flautist and composer J.J. Quantz. Bach may have been motivated to write his now famous *Essay on the True Art of Playing Keyboard Instruments* because his illustrious colleague was also working on a treatise, *On Playing the Flute* (1752). Both works are available in English translation and offer valuable insights into 18th-century performance practice.

Building a Musical Vocabulary: *Symphony*

Explain the importance of the following in terms of the origins and early development of the symphony:

Italian overture _____

_____

_____

rounded binary form _____

_____

_____

Sonata-Allegro form _____

_____

_____

Mannheim Orchestra _____

_____

_____

rocket theme _____

_____

_____

Identify two composers associated with the Mannheim School:

_____   _____

List four characteristic features that are associated with the Mannheim School:

1. use of long, gradual crescendo known as "Mannheim steamroller"
2. _____
3. _____
4. _____

Important among the contributions of the Pre-Classical composers was the development of Sonata-Allegro form. This formal structure served as the basis for the majority of Classical first movements. In the space provided below, draw a diagram outlining the standard components of Sonata-Allegro form, including key structure.

Define each of the following terms as they relate to the Classical symphony:

menuet and trio _____

scherzo _____

theme and variations _____

rondo _____

monothematic _____

The mature works of the Viennese masters demonstrate the standard four-movement structure that had evolved in the Pre-Classical years. Fill in the chart below to summarize the construction of a four-movement "sonata cycle."

Movement	Forms	Tempo	Musical Character
First	Sonata-Allegro	fast, lively	dramatic, energetic, spirited
Second			
Third			
Fourth			

Wolfgang Amadeus Mozart

Wolfgang Amadeus Mozart (1756-1791) explored virtually all the Classical genres that existed in his day, adding his personal stamp to each. In his symphonies, one can hear Mozart's operatic approach to melody, his command of orchestration and instrumental color, clarity of form, and innate natural beauty.

Required Listening: Mozart, *Symphony No. 40 in G Minor*, K 550

In 1788, in the remarkably short span of three months, Mozart completed his last three symphonies, Nos. 39, 40, and 41. Considered today to be some of the finest works in this genre, these symphonies were not performed in his lifetime. In many of Mozart's final compositions there is intensity, passion, and a compelling sense of urgency. These features are prevalent in *Symphony No. 40*, which is often designated as "The Romantic." This work is one of only two mature symphonies that Mozart wrote in minor keys.

Listen to a recording of *Symphony No. 40*. If possible, follow a score as you listen. Answer the questions below:

First Movement

Key _____   Form _____

Tempo _____   Meter _____

Exploring Music History: A Guided Approach

Exposition (mm. 1-100)

First Theme

Ex. 6.1. Mozart, *Symphony No. 40*, K 550, First Movement, mm. 1-9.

Which instruments are featured in the first theme? _____

How is this theme constructed? _____

What mood does the accompanying figure help create? _____

What is the dynamic indication here, and what is unusual about this?

Bridge

Ex. 6.2. Mozart, *Symphony No. 40*, K 550, First Movement, mm. 28-33.

How does Mozart create effective contrast with the bridge material?

Second Theme
Ex. 6.3. Mozart, *Symphony No. 40*, K 550, First Movement, mm. 44-51.

What is the new key of the second theme? _____

What are the featured instruments? _____

Identify three ways in which this theme contrasts with the first theme.

1. _____
2. _____
3. _____

Codetta
Ex. 6.4. Mozart, *Symphony No. 40*, K 550, First Movement, mm. 73-80.

How is the codetta related to the first theme?

_____
_____
_____
_____

Development (mm. 101-164)
In what unexpected key does the development section open? _____

Describe how material introduced earlier is treated in this section.

_____

_____

Which instruments create the effect of dialogue?

_____

_____

Recapitulation (mm. 165-299)

First theme key _____

Second theme key _____

When the second theme returns, how does the new key alter its character?

_____

What other changes are there in the recapitulation?

_____

How does the coda provide a definitive conclusion to this movement?

_____

To place your detailed study of the first movement into context, listen to the entire symphony and complete the chart below:

Movement	Key	Tempo	Meter	Form	Features
First					
Second					
Third					
Fourth					

Had Mozart lived longer, he may well have contributed further to the development of the symphonic repertoire. His untimely death at the age of thirty-five pre-empted the fulfillment of a contract he had with the impresario J.P. Salomon to unveil a set of new symphonies in London. By default, Salomon invited Haydn to come to England a second time. As a result of this invitation, Haydn produced his second set of "London Symphonies." Since these were his last works in this genre, we can speculate that without this opportunity, his final symphonies might not have been composed.

Franz Joseph Haydn

Franz Joseph Haydn (1732-1809) spent many years in the employ of the Esterházy princes. Their patronage provided him with ample opportunity to explore and perfect his approach to the symphonic genre. Both the Classical style and the make-up of the orchestra changed significantly between the time Haydn wrote his first and last symphonies.

Required Listening: Haydn, *Symphony No. 104 in D Major* ("London")

Symphony No. 104, composed in the twilight of Haydn's career, represents the culmination of years of experimentation and stylistic evolution. The use of a slow introduction, monothematic design, incorporation of folk elements, and the injection of humor and suspense are all hallmarks of Haydn's mature style.

Listen to a recording of *Symphony No. 104*. If possible, follow a score as you listen. Complete the outline below:

First Movement
Introduction ("Adagio," mm. 1-17)

Key _____   Tempo _____

Ex. 6.5. Haydn, *Symphony No. 104*, First Movement, "Adagio," mm. 1 and 2.

How is the key of the introduction related to the home key of the first movement?

_____

Describe the rhythmic character of the opening motive shown in Ex. 6.5.

_____

Which Baroque instrumental style does this figure resemble? _____

The texture of the opening is best described as _____.

As the introduction unfolds, the harmony becomes highly chromatic. Describe the mood or atmosphere that results.

_____

_____

_____

Exposition ("Allegro," mm. 1-107)

Key _____   Tempo _____

Meter _____

First Theme ("Allegro," mm. 1-15)
Ex. 6.6. Haydn, *Symphony No. 104*, First Movement, "Allegro," mm. 1-8.

Which instruments are featured in the first theme? _____

Describe how the musical character of this theme is created.

_____

_____

_____

Bridge ("Allegro," mm. 16-48)
Ex. 6.7. Haydn, *Symphony No. 104*, First Movement, "Allegro," mm. 16-19.

In what ways does the bridge contrast with the first theme?

_____

_____

Second Theme ("Allegro," mm. 49-83)

New key _____

Ex. 6.8. Haydn, *Symphony No. 104*, First Movement, "Allegro," mm. 66-73.

Which instruments are featured in the second theme? _____

Explain the relationship of the second theme to the first.

_____

_____

What term is used to denote this practice? _____

Codetta ("Allegro," mm. 84-107)

Ex. 6.9. Haydn, *Symphony No. 104*, First Movement, "Allegro," mm. 84-87.

What rhythmic device is used in the codetta, and what effect does it have on the mood?

_____

Development ("Allegro," mm. 108-176)

Opening key _____

What thematic materials are employed in the development section?

_____

_____

_____

How does Haydn build tension immediately before the recapitulation?

_____

_____

_____

Recapitulation ("Allegro," mm. 177-278)

Is the introduction heard again? _____

First theme key _____

Second theme key _____

How is the second theme embellished upon its return? _____
_____
_____

How does the coda create a rousing finale to this movement?
_____
_____

To place your detailed study of the first movement into context, listen to the entire symphony and complete the chart below:

Movement	Key	Tempo	Meter	Form	Features
First					
Second					
Third					
Fourth					

Conductors today arrive at different solutions regarding the observance of repeats in the exposition of Sonata-Allegro movements. What arguments can you put forward in support of observing the repeats?
_____
_____
_____

What justification would there be for ignoring the repeats?
_____
_____
_____

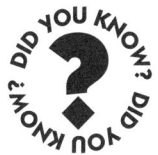

The symphonies of Haydn and Mozart served as a springboard for the genius of Beethoven. Although he composed only nine symphonies, Beethoven brought a wealth of innovative ideas to the genre. His five-movement *Symphony No. 6* ("Pastoral") challenged the traditional four-movement structure and is often cited as the first programmatic symphony. In his *Symphony No. 9* ("Choral"), Beethoven expanded the performing forces to include chorus and soloists. In using Schiller's celebrated *Ode to Joy* poem for that work, Beethoven articulated the hopes and dreams of his time: that all mankind can be united.

Recommended Listening for Symphony:
C.P.E Bach: *Symphony No. 3 in F Major*, H 665
F.J. Haydn: *Symphony No. 45* ("Farewell")
      Symphony No. 94 ("Surprise")
      Symphony No. 100 ("Military")
W.A. Mozart: *Symphony No. 35*, K 385 ("Haffner")
      Symphony No. 38, K 504 ("Prague")
      Symphony No. 41, K 551 ("Jupiter")
L. van Beethoven: *Symphony No. 3*, op. 55 ("Eroica")
      Symphony No. 6, op. 68 ("Pastoral")
      Symphony No. 9, op. 125 ("Choral")

Sonata

The Classical four-movement structure used in the symphony was also adapted to solo works, chamber music, and compositions for orchestra with soloist(s). The solo sonata, developed by Scarlatti earlier in the 18th century, evolved from a single-movement work to a multi-movement design. In this "sonata cycle," typically at least one movement used Sonata-Allegro form. The remaining movements provided contrast, which was achieved through changes in character, key, tempo, meter, and formal structure.

By the time of the Viennese masters, the popularity of the piano had eclipsed that of the earlier keyboard instruments. Haydn, Mozart, and Beethoven each produced numerous sonatas for the piano.

During Beethoven's lifetime, the piano underwent significant developments and improvements. Composers responded to the evolution of the instrument by exploiting the new sounds and colors. Piano-makers, in turn, were inspired by the increasingly virtuosic writing and continued to search for ways to refine the instrument. Using your search engine and the key words "Cristofori," "Silbermann," "Graf," and "Broadwood," have fun discovering more about the piano in Beethoven's time.

Ludwig van Beethoven

The thirty-two piano sonatas of Ludwig van Beethoven (1770-1827) are among the most important and influential works in the entire piano literature. Ranging from Opus 2 to Opus 111, these works illustrate Beethoven's stylistic development and evolution as he explored the sonata cycle in incredibly diverse ways. Listeners

Exploring Music History: A Guided Approach   Volume 2: Middle Ages to Classical

and concertgoers know some of the piano sonatas by their famous nicknames—
Moonlight, Tempest, Les Adieux, Appassionata, and *Pastoral.* Beethoven did not
provide most of these designations; in fact, he frowned upon several of them.

Required Listening: Beethoven, *Sonata in C Minor*, op. 13 ("Pathétique")

Beethoven did attach the subtitle "Pathétique" to his Opus 13 piano sonata.
Although it was written during his early style period, this work foreshadows the
turbulence and defiance present in many of Beethoven's middle period
compositions. A relationship can also be drawn to the *Sturm und Drang*
sentiments present in literary works of the day, which heralded the dawning of
the Romantic era.

What does the word "pathétique" convey to you?

_____

_____

_____

Listen to a recording or live performance of *Sonata in C Minor*, op. 13. Follow a
score while you listen. Complete the listening outline below:

First Movement

Key _____   Tempo _____

Meter _____

Introduction

Ex. 6.10. Beethoven, *Sonata in C Minor*, op. 13, First Movement, mm. 1 and 2.

How do each of the following musical elements contribute to the dramatic
atmosphere established in the Introduction?

rhythm _____

_____

_____

_____

texture _____

_____

_____

harmony _____

_____

_____

idiomatic writing _____

_____

_____

How does Beethoven create a rhapsodic, improvisatory character in this Introduction?

_____

_____

_____

Exposition

Key _____   Form _____

Tempo _____   Meter _____

First Theme

Ex. 6.11. Beethoven, *Sonata in C Minor*, op. 13, First Movement, mm. 11-19.

Describe the melodic shape and range of the right-hand part. How do these elements affect the musical character?

_____

_____

Describe how the left-hand accompaniment heightens the tension.

_____

_____

Bridge

Ex. 6.12. Beethoven, *Sonata in C Minor*, op. 13, First Movement, mm. 27-31.

From what thematic material is the bridge constructed? What tonal purpose does the bridge serve?

_____

_____

_____

Second Theme Group, Theme 2a

Ex. 6.13. Beethoven, *Sonata in C Minor*, op. 13, First Movement, mm. 51-59.

Name the key that was expected here. _____

What key was used instead? _____

What contributes to the agitated quality of this theme? _____

_____

Describe the technical challenge that this theme presents for the performer.

_____

_____

Second Theme Group, Theme 2b

Ex. 6.14. Beethoven, *Sonata in C Minor*, op. 13, First Movement, mm. 89-100.

What is the new key of this theme? _____

Describe the pianistic figuration used here. _____
_____
_____

Describe the harmonic progression. _____
_____

Codetta (m. 121)
On what material (heard previously) is the codetta based?
_____

Development (m. 133)
What thematic material opens the development? _____

In what key is this presented? _____

What unexpected modulation occurs in this opening passage? _____

At the return of *Allegro molto e con brio*, how has the key signature been altered?
_____

Which two themes are combined in this portion of the development?
_____

How does Beethoven create suspense and anticipation before the return of the first theme?
_____
_____

Recapitulation (m. 195)
Identify the key of the first theme in the recapitulation. _____

How has the bridge been altered? _____

In what unexpected key does Theme 2a reappear? _____

In what key does Theme 2b reappear? _____

Coda (m. 295)
What earlier material is presented for the last time at the coda, and how is it modified?
_____
_____

Exploring Music History: A Guided Approach   Volume 2: Middle Ages to Classical

What effect does this change have?

___

___

How does the movement come to a rousing conclusion?

___

___

Second Movement

Key _____   Form _____

Tempo _____   Meter _____

Section A
Ex. 6.15. Beethoven, *Sonata in C Minor*, op. 13, Second Movement, mm. 1-8.

How does Beethoven achieve a lyrical, hymn-like quality in this section?

___

___

What are the pianistic challenges posed by this opening passage?

___

___

___

Section B (m. 17)
In which key does this section begin? _____

To which key does it modulate? _____

How does this section create contrast with Section A?

___

___

___

Section A¹ (m. 29)
How is the return of Section A altered?

_____

Section C (m. 37)
In which key does this section begin? _____

What is the relationship of this new key to the tonic key of the movement?

_____

What new rhythmic figure is introduced here?

_____

To which key does this passage suddenly modulate? _____
(Enharmonic spelling of F flat major or "♭VI")

Section A² (m. 51)
How does this compare to the original Section A? What is the same, and what is different?

_____

_____

_____

Coda (m. 66)
How does the coda provide a fitting conclusion to this movement?

_____

_____

_____

Third Movement

Key _____   Form _____

Tempo _____   Meter _____

Section A
Ex. 6.16. Beethoven, *Sonata in C Minor*, op. 13, Third Movement, mm. 1-8.

In the list below, circle the musical elements that are present in Section A:
- broken-chord accompaniment
- tremolo octaves
- agitated character
- hand crossings
- grace-note figures

In what key is the perfect cadence that concludes Section A?
- a) tonic key
- b) dominant key
- c) relative major

Section B (m. 18)
This section begins in the key of _____ and modulates to the key of _____.

Within Section B, which of the following is used to create contrast?
- a) triplet figures
- b) temporary shift to chordal texture
- c) long scale passages in the left hand

Which of the following is used at the end of Section B?
- a) extended trill in the right hand
- b) descending scale passage leading to a fermata over dominant seventh harmony
- c) deceptive cadence

Section A (m. 62)
When Section A returns, is it altered or unaltered? _____

Section C (m. 79)

Key _____

In the list below, circle the musical elements that are present in Section C:
- variation technique
- syncopation
- reference to the "Grave" theme of the first movement
- dialogue between the hands
- extended descending staccato scale passages
- extended dominant preparation
- Alberti bass accompaniment

Section A^1 (m. 121)
How has Section A been altered?

_____

_____

Section B^2 (m. 134)
Section B^2 begins in the key of _____.

How is this section different from the original Section B?

_____

_____

_____

Section A² (m. 171)
How is this section different from the original Section A?

_____

_____

_____

Coda (m. 182)
What material heard previously is featured in the coda?

_____

_____

_____

To conclude your study of this sonata, summarize the three movements by filling in the chart below:

Movement	Key	Tempo	Meter	Form	Features
First					
Second					
Third					

Supplemental Activity: *Comparing Sonata Recordings*

The "Pathétique" Sonata is a very popular work that has been recorded by many concert artists. Interpretations vary widely. Listen to three recordings of this work performed by three different pianists, and record your impressions below:

Recording No. 1

Pianist _____

Recording label and date _____

Tempo _____

Dynamics _____

Observation of repeats _____

General impression/comments _____

_____

Recording No. 2

Pianist _____

Recording label and date _____

Tempo _____

Dynamics _____

Observation of repeats _____

General impression/comments _____

_____

Recording No. 3

Pianist _____

Recording label and date _____

Tempo _____

Dynamics _____

Observation of repeats _____

General impression/comments _____

_____

Which recording did you enjoy the most, and why?

_____

_____

_____

Recommended Listening for Sonata:
F.J. Haydn: *Sonata in E flat Major*, Hob. XVI:52
    Sonata in E Minor, Hob. XVI:34
W.A. Mozart: *Sonata in F Major*, K 332
    Sonata in B flat Major, K 333
L. van Beethoven: *Sonata in D Major*, op. 10, no. 3
    Sonata in C Major, op. 53 ("Waldstein")
    Sonata in E Major, op. 109

Sonatas in *Celebration Series®, The Piano Odyssey®*:
C.P.E. Bach: *Sonata in C Minor*, Wq48/4, H27 (*Piano Repertoire 9*)
F.J. Haydn: *Sonata in G Major*, Hob. XVI:27 (*Piano Repertoire 8*)
    Sonata in E Minor, Hob. XVI:34 (*Piano Repertoire 9*)
    Sonata in B Minor, Hob. XVI:32 (*Piano Repertoire 10*)
W.A. Mozart: *Sonata in C Major*, K 330 (*Piano Repertoire 9*)
    Sonata in E flat Major, K 282 (*Piano Repertoire 10*)
L. van Beethoven: *Sonata in G Major*, op. 49, no. 2 (*Piano Repertoire 8*)
    Sonata in G Major, op. 79 (*Piano Repertoire 9*)
    Sonata in E Major, op. 14, no. 1 (*Piano Repertoire 10*)

Concerto

Of the two types of Baroque concertos (solo concerto and concerto grosso), the solo concerto continued its evolution and absorbed the main currents of Classical style. In the hands of the Viennese masters, this three-movement work became a vehicle for virtuosity as well as an opportunity for experiments with musical architecture.

Building a Musical Vocabulary: *Classical Concerto*

Define each of the following terms as they relate to the Classical concerto:

double exposition _____

_____

_____

tutti _____

_____

_____

cadenza _____

_____

_____

cadential six-four chord _____

_____

_____

Wolfgang Amadeus Mozart

Mozart's compositional gifts shine through in his twenty-seven solo piano concertos. Since he was an extraordinarily gifted pianist, it is not surprising that he turned to this emerging idiom. Mozart himself was able to premiere the bulk of his piano concertos, performing as soloist/conductor. In these works, one can observe a stylistic evolution; each concerto displays new innovations in terms of structure and in the roles given to orchestra and soloist.

Required Listening: Mozart, *Piano Concerto in G Major*, K 453

Listen to a recording of the *Piano Concerto in G Major*, K 453. If possible, follow a score as you listen. Answer the questions below:

In what year was this concerto composed? _____

To whom was it dedicated? _____

Who was she? _____

First Movement

Key _____ Meter _____ Tempo _____

Form _____

Orchestral Exposition

First Theme

Ex. 6.17. Mozart, *Piano Concerto in G Major*, K 453, First Movement, mm. 1-5.

Describe the character of the first theme. _____

_____

Which instruments are featured? _____

How does the bridge theme provide contrast? _____

_____

Describe the character of the second theme. _____

_____

Which qualities are similar to the first theme, and which are a departure?

_____

Solo Exposition

First Theme
Ex. 6.18. Mozart, *Piano Concerto in G Major*, K 453, First Movement, mm. 74-78.

Describe the treatment of the thematic material when played by the soloist, and comment on the pianistic challenges.

_____

At m. 97, a transitional section begins. What musical events take place in this section?

_____

_____

Piano Theme
This theme was not heard in the orchestral exposition. What is its key? _____

Relationship to home key _____

Ex. 6.19. Mozart, *Piano Concerto in G Major*, K 453, First Movement, mm. 110-113.

What musical character is created in this passage? How is this achieved?

_____

_____

Which other instruments are featured, and what are their roles?

In what key does the second theme return, and how is it orchestrated?

Describe the closing section.

Development

What treatment is given to the themes in this section?

What new keys are used in the development, and how are they related?

What are the pianistic challenges in this section?

How did Mozart prepare the listener for the recapitulation?

Recapitulation

How does the thematic treatment and texture of the first theme differ in the recapitulation as compared to the exposition?

How have the other themes been altered?

Cadenza

Describe the cadenza in the recording you listened to. Who composed it? What thematic material was incorporated and how? What characters or moods did the performer convey?

Second Movement

Key _____   Relationship to home key _____

Meter _____   Tempo _____

Form _____

Why is this an unusual choice of form for the second movement in a Classical concerto?

_____

_____

Ex. 6.20. Mozart, *Piano Concerto in G Major*, K 453, Second Movement, mm. 1-5.

The role of the second movement in a Classical concerto is to create contrast with the outer movements while offering an opportunity for the soloist to display lyricism. Describe how this second movement achieves both of these objectives.

_____

_____

_____

_____

_____

While this movement adopts a formal structure similar to that of the first movement, it contains some interesting surprises. In the solo exposition, what unexpected key is boldly announced before the expected G major? _____

In what unexpected key does this theme reappear within the recapitulation? _____

Describe the performance of this movement's cadenza in the recording you listened to.

_____

_____

_____

Exploring Music History: A Guided Approach   Volume 2: Middle Ages to Classical

Third Movement

Key _____ Meter _____ Tempo _____

Form _____

Ex. 6.21. Mozart, *Piano Concerto in G Major*, K 453, Third Movement, mm. 1-8.

What musical character or mood is conveyed in the opening statement of the main theme?

_____

_____

What is the formal structure of the theme itself? _____

What type of phrase structure is employed? _____

Which instruments present the theme? _____

From the choices provided below, circle all the musical events that take place in each of the variations, and in the coda. (You may circle more than one event in each section.)

Variation 1
a) solo piano featured
b) woodwind triplets
c) frequent modulation
d) prominent use of appoggiaturas

Variation 2
a) piano triplet figures
b) brass fanfares
c) woodwind statement of theme
d) fugal texture

Variation 3
a) piano and strings in dialogue
b) theme varied rhythmically
c) solo woodwind instruments in dialogue
d) left-hand Alberti bass (piano)

Variation 4
- a) sense of mystery conveyed
- b) use of the tonic minor key
- c) emphasis on syncopation
- d) prominent use of chromaticism

Variation 5
- a) subdued character
- b) march for full orchestra
- c) extended piano trill
- d) prominent use of triplets

Coda
- a) change to *andante* tempo
- b) change to *presto* tempo
- c) pedal points featured
- d) virtuoso pianistic challenges

As you did for the first two movements, describe the performance of the cadenza in the recording you listened to.

_____

_____

_____

Supplemental Activity: *Sampling Additional Concertos*

Listen to a recording or a live performance of a Classical concerto for an instrument other than the piano, and then complete the following information:

Composer and title _____

Performer _____

Orchestra and conductor _____

Musical features _____

_____

_____

Personal impressions (reasons for enjoying the work and its interpretation).

_____

_____

_____

Recommended Listening for Concerto:
Beethoven: *Piano Concerto No. 4 in G Major*, op. 58
    Violin Concerto in D Major, op. 61
Mozart: *Piano Concerto in D Minor*, K 466
    Piano Concerto in C Major, K 467
    Clarinet Concerto in A Major, K 622
    Flute Concerto in G Major, K 313
Haydn: *Trumpet Concerto in E flat Major*

Chamber Music

Chamber music has been likened to "a musical conversation between friends." This genre enjoyed an increasingly greater significance in the Classical era. As amateur music-making grew in popularity in the 18th century, patrons not only sponsored works, but they were often active participants. Haydn, Mozart, and Beethoven created a large repertoire of chamber music and significantly advanced this genre. The next great Viennese master, Franz Schubert, also contributed many outstanding works. On several occasions, as in the "Trout" Quintet, Schubert drew inspiration from his own Lieder.

Building a Musical Vocabulary: *Chamber Music*

Define the following terms:

chamber music _____

_____

duo sonata (instrumental sonata) _____

_____

piano trio _____

_____

string trio _____

_____

string quartet _____

_____

piano quintet _____

_____

string quintet _____

_____

octet _____

_____

Franz Schubert

The last of the four great Viennese composers, Franz Schubert (1797-1828) stands as a transitional composer whose music exemplifies traits of both Classical and Romantic musical style. Although he is best known for his six hundred German Lieder, Schubert's output in the chamber music genre includes numerous masterpieces: fifteen string quartets, one string quintet, two piano trios, duo sonatas, one wind octet, and the famous "Trout" Quintet.

Required Listening: Schubert, *Piano Quintet in A Major* ("Trout")

In our exploration of music from the Middle Ages and Renaissance, we discovered that composers often based their instrumental works on vocal models. The "Trout" Quintet offers another example of this approach. Schubert beautifully adapted his own charming song, *Die Forelle* (the "Trout") and used it as the basis of the fourth movement of this quintet.

A striking element of the "Trout" Quintet is the instrumentation: piano, violin, viola, cello, and double bass. The double bass, not usually included in small chamber music ensembles, brings new coloristic and textural possibilities to the standard piano quartet sound. This combination of instruments is clearly a reason for the work's enduring appeal.

Fourth Movement

Schubert based this movement on *Die Forelle*, a song he composed in 1817. Prior to studying this quintet movement, listen to the original song.

Ex. 6.22. Schubert, *Die Forelle*, mm. 1-10.

What does the text of *Die Forelle* describe?

_____

_____

_____

How are the images of splashing water captured in the song's piano accompaniment?

_____

_____

Listen to a recording of the fourth movement of the "Trout" Quintet. If possible, follow a score as you listen. Answer the following questions:

Key _____   Meter _____   Tempo _____

Form _____

Theme

Ex. 6.23. Schubert, *Quintet in A Major* ("Trout"), Fourth Movement, mm. 1-8.

What is the instrumentation at the beginning of this movement?

_____

Which instrument carries the tune? _____

Describe the character. _____

What is the texture? _____

What is the formal structure of the theme?

_____

Fill in the requested information for each of the six variations. The first variation has been completed as an example.

Variation 1

Instrument(s) that play(s) the theme   *piano*

Musical character   *graceful, elegant*

Variation techniques employed   *theme embellished, ornamented with trills*

_____

Other special features   *low strings play pizzicato, violin plays trills, piano plays*

melody with both hands separated by an octave

Variation 2

Instrument(s) that play(s) the theme _____

Musical character _____

Variation techniques employed _____

_____

Other special features _____

_____

Variation 3

Instrument(s) that play(s) the theme _____

Musical character _____

Variation techniques employed _____

_____

Other special features _____

_____

Variation 4

Instrument(s) that play(s) the theme _____

Musical character _____

Variation techniques employed _____

_____

Other special features _____

_____

Variation 5

Instrument(s) that play(s) the theme _____

Musical character _____

Variation techniques employed _____

_____

Other special features _____

_____

Variation 6

Instrument(s) that play(s) the theme _____

Musical character _____

_____

Variation techniques employed _____

Other special features _____

_____

To conclude your study of this quintet, listen to the complete work and summarize the five movements by filling in the chart below:

Movement	Key	Tempo	Meter	Form	Features
First					
Second					
Third					
Fourth					
Fifth					

Recommended Listening for Chamber Music:
Schubert: *Quintet for Strings in C Major*, D 956 ("Cello")
    String Quartet in D Minor, D 810 ("Death and the Maiden")
Mozart: *Piano Quintet in E flat Major*, K 452
    Piano Quartet in G Minor, K 478
Beethoven: *Piano Trio in D Major*, op. 70 ("Ghost")
    Piano Trio in B flat Major, op. 97 ("Archduke")
Mendelssohn: *Octet in E flat Major*, op. 20

Review and Reflection

From your own repertoire or music library, choose a work by one of the composers in this unit (Haydn, Mozart, Beethoven, or Schubert). Compare it to the required work in this unit by the same composer. First, list at least four style traits that were present in the required work. Then consider the piece you chose. Which of those features are also present?

Composer _____

Required work	**Work from your repertoire/library**
_____	_____

Style traits

e.g., employs Sonata-Allegro form	Sonata-Allegro form also used
_____	_____
_____	_____
_____	_____
_____	_____

Of the works you studied in this unit, which did you enjoy the most, and why?

_____

_____

_____

_____

_____

_____

_____

_____

_____

_____

Quiz

1. Name the composer and title of one Classical composition associated with each of the following. Draw your examples from the works you studied in this unit.

	Composition	**Composer**
Inclusion of choir and soloists	Symphony No. 9	Beethoven
Monothematic		
Menuet and trio		
Expanded coda		
Use of folk elements		
Programmatic elements		
Slow introduction		
Double exposition		
London premieres		
Theme and variations		
Rondo		

2. Name four ways in which Mozart contributed to the development of the concerto:

   1. _____
   2. _____
   3. _____
   4. _____

3. Name at least one composer from the Classical period who composed the following:

   Trumpet Concerto _____

   Horn Concerto _____

   Clarinet Concerto _____

   Violin Concerto _____

   Cello Concerto _____

   Triple Concerto for Violin, Cello, and Piano _____

4. Name four composers of keyboard concertos:

   _____   _____

   _____   _____

Final Review and Summary

Part One: Style Summary

Provide a point-form comparison of musical styles in the four eras you studied in this course.

	Middle Ages	Renaissance	Baroque	Classical
Approximate dates				
Significant historical events				
Leading centers or "schools"				
Major genres cultivated				
Principal composers				
Musical characteristics: Rhythm				
Texture				
Melody				
Formal structure				
Harmony				
Compositional devices				

Exploring Music History: A Guided Approach

Part Two: Personal Reflection

Of the musical genres you encountered in this course, which did you personally find most interesting and enjoyable to study, and why?

_____
_____
_____
_____
_____

Of the composers you studied in this course, whose music did you enjoy most? Who would you select if you had to choose only one of these composers as a favorite, and why?

_____
_____
_____
_____
_____

Of the four musical eras you studied, which musical style did you enjoy most overall? Which style will you most likely continue exploring after completing this course?

_____
_____
_____
_____
_____

Part Three: Timeline Summary

Now that you have completed your study of vocal and instrumental genres from the Middle Ages through the Classical era, place all of the genres you have explored and the composers you have discovered on the appropriate points on the timeline provided.

Final Review and Summary

Include all of the following in the timeline below:

Genres:
Cantata, Chamber Music, Chanson, Concerto, Dance Music, Gregorian Chant, Keyboard Music, Madrigal, Mass, Motet, Opera, Oratorio, Organum, Sonata, Suite, Symphony.

Composers:
d'Arras, C.P.E. Bach, J.S. Bach, Beethoven, de Vitry, Gesualdo, Gregory the Great, Gluck, Handel, Haydn, Hildegard of Bingen, des Prez, Farmer, Florentine Camerata, Franco-Flemish composers, Léonin, Machaut, Monteverdi, Mozart, Notre Dame School, Palestrina, Pérotin, Purcell, Scarlatti, Schubert, Susato, Viennese School.

A.D. 476	MIDDLE AGES	1450	RENAISSANCE	1600	BAROQUE	1750	CLASSICAL
GENRES							
COMPOSERS							

Exploring Music History: A Guided Approach   Volume 2: Middle Ages to Classical

Appendices

APPENDIX A — RECOMMENDED RESOURCES

Dictionaries and Encyclopedias

Chwialkowski, Jerzy. *The Da Capo Catalogue of Classical Music Compositions*. New York: Da Capo Press, 1996.

Kallmann, Helmut, Gilles Potvin, and Kenneth Winters, eds. *Encyclopedia of Music in Canada*. 2nd ed. Toronto: University of Toronto Press, 1992.

Kennedy, Michael, ed. *The Concise Oxford Dictionary of Music*. 4th ed. London: Oxford University Press, 1996.

Kennedy, Michael, ed. *The Oxford Dictionary of Music*. 2nd ed. London: Oxford University Press, 1995.

Randel, Don Michael, ed. *The Harvard Concise Dictionary of Music and Musicians*. Cambridge, Massachusetts: Belknap Press of Harvard University Press, 1999.

Randel, Don Michael, ed. *The New Harvard Dictionary of Music*. Cambridge, Massachusetts: Harvard University Press, 1986.

Sadie, Stanley, ed. *The New Grove Dictionary of Music and Musicians*. 2nd ed. 29 vols. London: Macmillan, 2001.

Sadie, Stanley, ed. *The New Grove Dictionary of Opera*. 4 vols. London: Macmillan, 1992.

Sadie, Stanley, ed. *The Norton/Grove Concise Encyclopedia of Music*. New York: W.W. Norton, 1988.

Slonimsky, Nicholas. *Baker's Biographical Dictionary of Musicians*. 8th ed. New York: Schirmer, 1984.

Slonimsky, Nicholas, and Laura Diane Kuhn. *Baker's Biographical Dictionary of Musicians*. 6 vols. Centennial ed. New York: Schirmer, 2001.

Westrup, Jack Allan et al. *The New College Encyclopedia of Music*. New York: W.W. Norton, 1981.

General Texts

Abraham, Gerald, ed. *The Concise Oxford History of Music*. London: Oxford University Press, 1985.

Gillespie, John. *Five Centuries of Keyboard Music: An Historical Survey of Music for Harpsichord and Piano*. Belmont, California: Wadsworth, 1965.

Grout, Donald Jay, and Claude V. Palisca. *A History of Western Music*. 6th ed. New York: W.W. Norton, 2001.

Grout, Donald J. *A Short History of Opera*. 3rd ed. New York: Columbia University Press, 1988.

Hanning, Barbara Rusanno. *A Concise History of Western Music*. 2nd ed. New York: W.W. Norton, 2002.

Holoman, D. Kern. *Masterworks: A Musical Discovery*. 2nd ed. Upper Saddle River, New Jersey: Prentice Hall, 2001.

Kirby, Frank E. *Music For Piano: A Short History*. Portland, Oregon: Amadeus Press, 1995.

Machlis, Joseph, and Kristine Forney. *The Enjoyment of Music*. 9th ed. New York: W.W. Norton, 2002.

Schonberg, Harold C. *Lives of the Great Composers*. 3rd ed. New York: W.W. Norton, 1997.

Stolba, K. Marie. *The Development of Western Music: A History*. 3rd ed. Boston, Massachusetts: McGraw-Hill, 1998.

Yudkin, Jeremy. *Understanding Music*. Upper Saddle River, New Jersey: Prentice Hall, 1999.

Middle Ages Texts

Bogin, Meg. *The Women Troubadours*. New York: W.W. Norton, 1980.

Hoppin, Richard H. *Medieval Music*. New York: W.W. Norton, 1978.

Hughes, Andrew. *Medieval Music: The Sixth Liberal Art*. Toronto: University of Toronto Press, 1980.

McKinnon, James, ed. *Source Readings in Music History: The Early Christian Period and the Latin Middle Ages*. Oliver Strunk, ed. Revised edition. New York: W.W. Norton, 1998.

Munrow, David. *Instruments of the Middle Ages and Renaissance.* London: Oxford University Press and EMI Records, 1976.

Reese, Gustave. *Music in the Middle Ages.* New York: W.W. Norton, 2000.

Seay, Albert. *Music in the Medieval World.* 2nd ed. Englewood Cliffs, New Jersey: Prentice-Hall, 1975.

Renaissance Period Texts

Atlas, Allan W. *Renaissance Music: Music in Western Europe, 1400-1600.* New York: W.W. Norton, 1998.

Blume, Friedrich. *Renaissance and Baroque Music: A Comprehensive Survey.* Trans. M.D. Herter. New York: W.W. Norton, 1967.

Brown, Howard M. *Music in the Renaissance.* Englewood Cliffs, New Jersey: Prentice-Hall, 1976.

Reese, Gustave. *Music in the Renaissance.* Revised edition. New York: W.W. Norton, 1959.

Tomlinson, Gary, ed. *Source Readings in Music History: The Renaissance.* Oliver Strunk, ed. Revised edition. New York: W.W. Norton, 1998.

Baroque Period Texts

Arnold, Denis, et al. *The New Grove Italian Baroque Masters: Monteverdi, Frescobaldi, Cavalli, Corelli, A. Scarlatti, Vivaldi, D. Scarlatti.* New York: W.W. Norton, 1997.

Boyd, Malcolm. *J.S. Bach.* London: Oxford University Press, 1999.

Bukofzer, Manfred. *Music in the Baroque Era: From Monteverdi to Bach.* New York: W.W. Norton, 1947.

David, Hans T., and Arthur Mendel, eds. *The New Bach Reader.* Revised and enlarged by Christoph Wolff. New York: W.W. Norton, 1999.

Hogwood, Christopher. *Handel.* New York: W.W. Norton, 1996.

Kirkpatrick, Ralph. *Domenico Scarlatti.* Princeton, New Jersey: Princeton University Press, 1981.

Landon, H.C. Robbins. *Handel and His World.* Boston: Little, Brown, 1984.

Murata, Margaret, ed. *Source Readings in Music History: The Baroque Era.* Oliver Strunk, ed. Revised edition. New York: W.W. Norton, 1998.

Palisca, Claude V. *Baroque Music.* 3rd ed. Englewood Cliffs, New Jersey: Prentice-Hall, 1991.

Wolff, Christoph. *Johann Sebastian Bach: The Learned Musician.* New York: W.W. Norton, 2000.

Wolff, Christoph, et al. *The New Grove Bach Family.* New York: W.W. Norton, 1997.

Classical Period Texts

Allanbrook, Wye J., ed. *Source Readings in Music History: The Late Eighteenth Century.* Oliver Strunk, ed. Revised edition. New York: W.W. Norton, 1998.

Blume, Friedrich. *Classic and Romantic Music.* Trans. M.D. Herter. New York: W.W. Norton, 1970.

Cooper, Barry. *The Beethoven Compendium: A Guide to Beethoven's Life and Music.* New York: W.W. Norton, 1996.

Deutsch, Otto Erich. *Mozart: A Documentary Biography.* Stanford: Stanford University Press, 1991.

Downs, Philip G. *Classical Music: The Era of Haydn, Mozart and Beethoven.* New York: W.W. Norton, 1992.

Geiringer, Karl. *Haydn: A Creative Life in Music.* 3rd ed., revised and expanded. Berkeley: University of California Press, 1983.

Hamburger, Michael, ed. *Beethoven's Letters, Journals, and Conversations.* New York: W.W. Norton, 1992.

Heartz, Daniel. *Haydn, Mozart and the Viennese School, 1740-1780.* New York: W.W. Norton, 1995.

Heartz, Daniel. *Music in the European Capitals, 1720-1780: The Galant Style.* New York: W.W. Norton, 2002.

Kerman, Joseph, Alan Tyson, et al. *The New Grove Beethoven.* New York: W.W. Norton, 1997.

Landon, H.C. Robbins. *Haydn: The Early Years, 1732-1765.* New York: W.W. Norton, 1995.

Landon, H.C. Robbins. *Haydn: At Esterházy, 1766-1790.* New York: W.W. Norton, 1995.

Landon, H.C. Robbins. *Haydn in England, 1791-1795.* New York: W.W. Norton, 1995.

Landon, H.C. Robbins. *Haydn: The Years of "The Creation."* New York: W.W. Norton, 1995.

Landon, H.C. Robbins. *Haydn: The Late Years, 1801-1809.* New York: W.W. Norton, 1995.

Newman, William S. *Beethoven on Beethoven: Playing His Piano Music His Way.* New York: W.W. Norton, 1991.

Newman, William S. *The Sonata in the Classical Era.* 3rd ed. New York: W.W. Norton, 1983.

Pauly, Reinhard G. *Music in the Classic Period.* 4th ed. Upper Saddle River, New Jersey: Prentice Hall, 2000.

Ratner, Leonard G. *Classic Music: Expression, Form and Style.* New York: Schirmer, 1980.

Rosen, Charles. *The Classical Style: Haydn, Mozart and Beethoven.* Expanded edition. New York: W.W. Norton, 1998.

Solomon, Maynard. *Mozart: A Life.* New York: Harper Collins Publishers, 1995.

Solomon, Maynard. *Beethoven.* New York: Schirmer Books, 1977.

Spaethling, Robert, ed. *Mozart's Letters, Mozart's Life: Selected Letters.* New York: W.W. Norton, 2000.

Till, Nicholas. *Mozart and the Enlightenment: Truth, Virtue, and Beauty in Mozart's Operas.* New York: W.W. Norton, 1996.

Zaslaw, Neal, and William Cowdery, eds. *The Complete Mozart: A Guide to the Musical Works of Wolfgang Amadeus Mozart.* New York: W.W. Norton, 1990.

Internet Resources (General Sites)

Worldwide Internet Music Resources:
www.music.indiana.edu/music_resources

Sibelius Academy Music Resources:
www.siba.fi/Kulttuuripalvelut/music.html

The Classical Music Pages:
www.rz-berlin.mpg.de/cmp/classmus.html

Classical Net:
www.classical.net

Listen (Kerman/Tomlinson):
www.bedfordstmartins.com/listen

VHS Video Resources

The Famous Composers Series. Written, produced, and directed by Malcolm Hossick. Titles include: *Johann Sebastian Bach, Ludwig van Beethoven, Joseph Haydn, Wolfgang Amadeus Mozart, Franz Schubert.* (Distributed by Kultur)

A & E "Biography" Series. *Mozart and Beethoven: The Sound and The Fury.* (Distributed by New Video)

The Story of the Symphony. With André Previn and The Royal Philharmonic. Six-part Series. Vol. 1: Haydn and Mozart, Vol. 2: Beethoven. (Distributed by Kultur)

BACH:

Glenn Gould Series, Sony 48403, 48404, 48405, 48406, 48408, 48409, 48433

Whole Notes – Bach: Serving God, the Music, Jon Kimura Parker, Pinchas Zukerman, conductor, Kultur 2044

MOZART:

Le nozze di Figaro, Fischer-Dieskau/Dietrich/Te Kanawa/Freni/Prey/Ewing/Böhm, directed by Ponnelle, DG 072553 3

Live in Italy, Cecilia Bartoli, Decca 440 074 204 3

Portrait, Cecilia Bartoli, Decca 071 241 3

Kiri Sings Mozart, Kiri Te Kanawa, EMI (VHS) MVC 991242 3

Mozart: Mitsuko Uchida, Salzburg Mozarteum, Philips 070241

DVD Video Resources

GESUALDO: Death for Five Voices, directed by Werner Herzog, Image Entertainment ID9330RADVD

MONTEVERDI: *The Coronation of Poppea*

Schumann/Croft, Concerti Koln, conducted by René Jacobs, Arhaus 1000109

MOZART: *Le nozze di Figaro*

Pape/Roschmanal/Magee/Trekel, Staatskapelle Berlin, conducted by Daniel Barenboim, Arthaus 100017

Furlanetti/Szymtka, Opera National de Lyon, conducted by Paolo Olmi, Kultur D 1484

HANDEL: *Water Music*
Capella Istropolitana, Warchal, Naxos DVDI 0992

HAYDN: *Symphony No. 104*
Capella Istropolitana, Wordsworth, Naxos 1007

MOZART: *Symphony No. 40*
Capella Istropolitana, Wordsworth, Naxos 0994

Picardy Sinfonietta, Patrick Fournillier, Image Entertainment ID5087GCDVD

APPENDIX B — RECOMMENDED LISTENING MATERIALS

The following is a list of suggested recordings for each of the required pieces discussed in this volume:

General (Anthologies)

- *The Enjoyment of Music*, 8th ed. (Machlis/Fornay), Sony Music Special Products ABA 34011

    Volume 1:
    Haec dies (chant and organum); *O mitissima-Virgo-Haec dies*; *Ave maria...virgo serena*; *Gloria* from *Missa Papae Marcelli*; *Ce fut en mai*; *Puis qu'en oubli*; *Fair Phyllis*; *The Coronation of Poppea* (Act 3, Scene 7); *Dido and Aeneas* (Act 3, Final Scene); *The Marriage of Figaro* (Act 1, Scenes 6-7); Cantata No. 80 (First, Second, Fifth, and Eighth Movements); *The Creation* (Part 1, Scene 3); *Royal Estampie No. 4*; *Water Music* (*Allegro* and *Hornpipe*); *Brandenburg Concerto No. 2 in F Major* (First and Second Movements); *Symphony No. 40 in G Minor* (First Movement); *Piano Concerto in G Major*, K 453 (complete); *Piano Sonata*, op. 13 ("Pathétique") (complete)

    Volume 2:
    Piano Quintet in D Major ("Trout") (Fourth Movement)

- *The Development of Western Music*, 3rd ed. (Stolba), Sony Music Special Products 0-697-32872-4
    Volume 1:
    Ave Maria...virgo serena; *Moro lasso*: *Dido and Aeneas* (Act 3, Final Scene)

UNIT TWO: Sacred Vocal Music of the Middle Ages and Renaissance

Hildegard of Bingen
- *Gothic Voices*, directed by Christopher Page, Hyperion CDA 20039
- *Vox Animae*, Mayfield Chamber Opera Chorus and Soloists, directed by Michael Fields and Evelyn Tubb, Etcetera KTC 1203

Notre Dame School
- *Music of the Gothic Era*, Early Music Consort of London, directed by David Munrow, Archiv 415 292-2
- *The Age of Cathedrals*, Theatre of Voices, directed by Paul Hillier, Harmonia Mundi HMU 907157
- *Magister Leoninus*, Red Byrd/Capella Amsterdam, Hyperion 66944
- *Pérotin*, The Hilliard Ensemble, directed by Paul Hillier, ECM 837 751-2
- *Josquin des Prez: Ave Maria*, Theatre of Voices, directed by Paul Hillier, Harmonia Mundi HMU 907136
- *Giovanni Pierluigi da Palestrina: Missa Papae Marcelli*, Westminster Cathedral Choir, directed by David Hill, Hyperion CDA 66266
- Regensberger Domspatzen, Ratzinger, EMI HM 7 47528 2
- Wiener Motetenchor, Klebel, Christophorus CD 74512

UNIT THREE: Secular Vocal Music of the Middle Ages and Renaissance

Moniot d'Arras: *Ce fut en mai*
- *Songs of Chivalry*, Martin Best Medieval Ensemble, Nimbus NI 5006

Guillaume de Machaut: *Puis qu'en oubli*
- *Songs from Le voir dit*, Oxford Camerata, directed by Jeremy Summerly, Naxos 8.553833
- *Le vrai remède d'amour*, Ensemble Gilles Binchois, directed by Dominique Velard, Cantus C 9625
- *A Distant Mirror*, The Folger Consort, Delos DE 1003

Carlo Gesualdo: *Moro lasso*
- *O dolorosa gioia,* Concerto Italiano, directed by Rinaldo Alessandri, Opus 111 OPS 30 238
- *Principe di Verona: Madrigals, Book 6*, Ensemble Métamorphoses, directed by Maurice Bourbon, Arion ARN 68389
- *Pavaniglia: Dances & Madrigals from 17th Century Italy*, King's Noyse, directed by David Douglass, HMU 907246

John Farmer: *Fair Phyllis I Saw Sitting All Alone*
- *All at once well met*, The King's Singers, EMI CDC7 49265-2

UNIT FOUR: Vocal Music of the Baroque and Classical Eras

Claudio Monteverdi: *The Coronation of Poppea*
- Donath/Soderstrom/Berberian/Lucciardi, Vienna Concentus Musicus, conducted by Nikolaus Harnoncourt, Teldec 2292-42547-2
- McNair/Von Otter/Hanchard/Chance, The English Baroque Soloists, conducted by John Eliot Gardiner, Archiv 447-088-2
- Borst/Laurens/Larmore/Schopper, Concerto Vocale, directed by Rene Jacobs, Harmonia Mundi HMC 90 1330/2

Henry Purcell: *Dido and Aeneas*
- von Otter/Varcoe/Dawson/Rogers, The English Concert and Choir, conducted by Trevor Pinnock, Archiv 427-624-2
- Baker/Herincx/Clark/Sinclair, The St. Anthony Singers, English Chamber Orchestra, conducted by Anthony Lewis, Decca 425 720-2
- Laurens/Feldman/Cantor, Les Arts Florissants, directed by William Christie, HMC 905173

Christoph Willibald Gluck: *Orphée et Euridice*
- von Otter/Hendricks/Fournier, Monteverdi Choir, Orchestre de l'Opera de Lyon, directed by John Eliot Gardiner, EMI CDS 556885 2

Mozart: *The Marriage of Figaro*
- Ramey/Popp/Allen/Te Kanawa/von Stade, London Opera Chorus, London Philharmonic Orchestra, conducted by Sir George Solti, Decca 410 150-2
- Terfel/Hagley/Martinpelto/Gilfry/Stephen, The Monteverdi Choir, English Baroque Soloists, conducted by Sir John Eliot Gardiner, Archiv 439871-2
- Siepi/Gueden/Poell/Della Casa/Danco, Vienna State Opera Chorus, conducted by Erich Kleiber, DECCA 417-315-2
- Allemans/Antonacci/Bartoli/D'Arcangelo, Vienna State Opera Chorus, Vienna Philharmonic Orchestra, conducted by Claudio Abbado, DG 445 903-2
- Wixell/Norman/Freni/Ganzarolli/Minton, BBC Symphony Orchestra and Chorus, conducted by Sir Colin Davis, Philips 422 540-2
- Allen/Price/Battle/Hynninen, Konzertvereinigung Wiener Staatsopernchor, Wiener Philharmoniker, conducted by Riccardo Muti, EMI CDS 747978 8
- Fischer-Dieskau/Harper/Blegen/Evans/Berganza, John Aldis Choir, English Chamber Orchestra, conducted by Daniel Barenboim, EMI CZS 572230 2

Johann Sebastian Bach: *Cantata No. 80*
- Ameling/Baldin/Ramey, London Voices, English Chamber Orchestra, conducted by Raymond Leppard, Philips 422 490-2
- Fontana/Winbergh/Krause/Hymnuschor, Stuttgarter Kammerorchester, conducted by Karl Münchinger, London 414 045-2
- Geraint Jones Singers, South German Madrigal Choir, Consortium Musicum conducted by Wolfgang Gonnenwein, EMI 7243 5 68670 2 4
- Bach Collegium Japan, conducted by Masaaki Suzuki, BIS CD 1151 1152
- Bryden/Minter/Thomas/Opalach, The Bach Ensemble, conducted by Joshua Rifkin, L'Oiseau-Lyre 455 706-2

Franz Joseph Haydn: *The Creation*
- Janowitz/Ludwig/Wunderlich/Krenn/Fischer-Dieskau, Wiener Singverein, Berliner Philharmoniker, conducted by Herbert von Karajan, DG 449 761-2
- Mathis/Jerusalem/Fischer-Dieskau, Academy of St. Martin-in-the-Fields, conducted by Neville Marriner, Philips 438 715-2
- Upshaw/Humphrey/Cheek/Murphy/McGuire, Atlanta Symphony and Chorus, conducted by Robert Shaw, Telarc CD 80298
- Popp/Dose/Hollweg/Mull/Luxon, Brighton Festival Chorus, Royal Philharmonic Orchestra, conducted by Antal Dorati, London 443 027-2
- Auger/Langridge/Thomas, City of Birmingham Chorus and Orchestra, conducted by Simon Rattle, EMI CDS 754159-2

UNIT FIVE: Instrumental Music of the Middle Ages, Renaissance, and Baroque

Tielman Susato: *Danserye*
- Musica Antiqua Ensemble, directed by Pierre Vereny, PV 785022
- *Carlos V*, La Capella Royal de Catalunya Hespèrion XXI, conducted by Jordi Savall, Alia Vox AV 9814
- Collegium Vocale, directed by Wolfgang Fromme, CBS M2YK 45622
- *Byrd: Virginals and Consorts*, Capriccio Stravgante, Astrée E 8611

- *At the Sign of the Crumhorn: Flemish Songs and Dance Music from the Susato Music Books,* Naxos 8.554425
- *Full Well She Sang: Women's Music from the Middle Ages and Renaissance,* The Toronto Consort, SR1005

Fitzwilliam Virginal Book
- Ursula Deutschler, Claves CD 50-9001

Domenico Scarlatti: *Sonata in D Minor,* L 413/K 9; *Sonata in D Major,* L 463/K 430
- *Celebration Series®, The Piano Odyssey®* (CD Level 9)
- *Best Sonatas,* Scott Ross, Erato 2292 45423 2
- Ivo Pogorelich, DG 435 855-2
- *The Baroque Album,* John Williams, CBS LMYK 42538
- Colin Tilney, Dorian DOR 90103

George Frideric Handel: *Water Music (Orchestral Suite in D Major)*
- The English Concert, conducted by Trevor Pinnock, Archiv 410 525-2
- English Baroque Soloists, conducted by John Eliot Gardiner, Philips 434 122-2
- Philharmonia Baroque Orchestra, conducted by Nicholas McGegan, Harmonia Mundi HCX 3957010
- Berliner Philharmoniker, conducted by Riccardo Muti, EMI CDR 569809 2
- Academy of St. Martin-in-the-Fields, conducted by Neville Marriner, EMI CDC 749810 2

J.S. Bach: *Brandenburg Concerto No. 2 in F Major,* BWV 1047
- Amsterdam Baroque Orchestra, conducted by Ton Koopman, Erato 4509 91930-2
- Concentus Musicus Wien, conducted by Nikolaus Harnoncourt, Teldec 4509-95980-2
- Academy of St. Martin-in-the-Fields, conducted by Neville Marriner, EMI CDR 569877 2
- Polish Chamber Orchestra, conducted by Jerzy Maksymiuk, EMI CZS 569749 2

UNIT SIX: Instrumental Music of the Classical Era

Franz Joseph Haydn: *Symphony No. 104 in D Major* ("London")
- Royal Concertgebouw Orchestra, conducted by Sir Colin Davis, Philips 464 707 2
- Royal Philharmonic Orchestra, conducted by Sir Thomas Beecham, EMI CMS7 64066-2
- Orchestra of the 18th Century, conducted by Frans Bruggen, Philips 442 7 88-2
- Collegium Musicum 90, conducted by Richard Hickox, Chandos CHAN 065
- Vienna Symphony Orchestra, conducted by Jascha Horenstein, VOX 2 7806 (includes *The Creation*)
- Berliner Philharmoniker, conducted by Herbert von Karajan, EMI CDM 566097 2
- English Chamber Orchestra, conducted by Jeffrey Tate, EMI CDR 572970 2

Wolfgang Amadeus Mozart: *Symphony No. 40 in G Minor,* K 550
- Columbia Symphony Orchestra, conducted by Bruno Walter, Sony SM3K 46511
- Cleveland Orchestra, conducted by George Szell, CBS MK 44518
- Collegium Aureum, conducted by Franz-Josef Maier, Pro Arte CDD 233
- English Chamber Orchestra, conducted by Jeffrey Tate, EMI CDC 7 47147 2
- Academy of St. Martin-in-the-Fields, conducted by Neville Marriner, EMI CDC 7 49703 2
- Berliner Philharmoniker, conducted by Herbert von Karajan, EMI CDM 566100 2

Ludwig van Beethoven: *Piano Sonata in C Minor,* op. 13 ("Pathétique")
- Emil Gilels, DG 400 036-2
- Arthur Rubinstein, BMG 09026 63010-2
- Alfred Brendel, Philips 438 730-2
- Claudio Arrau, Philips 420 153-2
- Rudolf Serkin, CBS LMYK 42539
- Vladimir Ashkenazy, London 436 380-2
- Anton Kuerti, Analekta FL 2 3007

Wolfgang Amadeus Mozart: *Piano Concerto in G Major,* K 453
- Richard Goode, Orpheus Chamber Orchestra, Nonesuch 79042-2
- Murray Perahia, English Chamber Orchestra, CBS 36686
- Alfred Brendel, Academy of St. Martin-in-the-Fields, conducted by Neville Marriner, Philips 422507-2
- Angela Cheng, CBC Orchestra, conducted by Mario Bernardi, CBC SMCD 5104

Franz Schubert: *Piano Quintet in D Major,* D 667 ("Trout")
- Ax/Frank/Young/Ma/Meyer, Sony SK 61964
- Emil Gilels, Amadeus Quartet, DG 449 746-2
- Sviatoslav Richter, Borodin Quartet, EMI CDC 7 47009 2
- Elisabeth Leonskaja, Alban Berg Quartet, EMI CDC 747448 2
- Emanuel Ax, Guarneri Quartet, BMG 09026 63589 2
- Jeno Jando, Kodály Quartet, Naxos 8550658

APPENDIX C — LISTENING REPORT

We recommend that students listen to additional works besides those studied in detail. Teachers may wish to use this listening report template to make weekly listening assignments from the recommended listening lists provided for each composer studied.

Title _____

Composer _____

Genre _____

Approximate date of composition _____

Recording or performance:

    Artist _____

    Label _____

Performing forces _____

Construction/number of movements _____

Summarize your impressions of this recording or performance by writing a brief review.

_____

_____

_____

_____

_____

_____

_____

_____

_____

_____

Notes

Notes

Notes

Notes